The Catch
And
The Feast

The Catch
And
The Feast

by Joie and Bill McGrail
Photography by Mark Shaw

Weybright and Talley
New York

Art Direction and Design:
Samuel N. Antupit
Editorial Consultation:
Dick Harrison

All photographs in
The Catch And The Feast
were taken with Nikon
cameras and Nikkor lenses.

Published in the
United States by
Weybright and Talley, Inc.
3 East 54th Street
New York, New York 10022

Published simultaneously
in Canada by
Clarke, Irwin & Company Limited
Toronto and Vancouver

Library of Congress Catalog
Card Number: 73-85153

Printed in the
United States of America

Illustrations printed in
The Netherlands

Table of Contents

Preface

The Catch And The Feast *is the story of our romance with rivers and marshes, oceans and lakes, mountains and woodlands, meadows and fields. It is a joyous kaleidoscope of shared experience in which each new adventure expands both self and mutual awareness. We brought quite different attitudes to our first hunt together. Bill had been a lifelong hunter; Joie had never been in the field. The deep contentment Bill found in testing himself against the primeval obstacles of the chase and the ancient instinct to harvest his sustenance for himself was completely foreign to Joie. These different outlooks were both essential to the completion of this book. It was written from Joie's perspective of growing appreciation and awareness of the pleasures and fulfillment of this timeless pursuit, based on the knowledge and understanding of Bill's years of experience. Our lives and our relationship have been immeasurably enriched by our involvement in the entire process of the catch and the feast. We hope that our readers will share this basic satisfaction with us.*

Joie and Bill McGrail

Acknowledgments

Our sincere appreciation
for their assistance
and cooperation to:
Sam Sako
Robert Puglisi
Karin Shakery
Schuyler Van Vechten, Jr.
Cliff Morrow
E. S. McCawley, Jr.
Dr. Robert F. Hutton
Anthony S. Taormina
Joel Arrington
Ethel and John Trenga
Jane and Bob Senior
Captain Geb Martin

Special Acknowledgment

Our deepest appreciation to
Dick Harrison
without whose assistance
this book could not
have been written.

The Catch
And
The Feast

Chapter 1.
Deer Hunt à Deux

About two weeks after marrying Bill I got an extraordinary surprise. This marvelously cosmopolitan man, who had courted me in dinner jacket at New York's most elegant restaurants and entertainments, asked, "How would you like to go hunting?" The question was nonchalant, but it was all too apparent that I was to undergo a monumental change in my life style.

"Hunting" was the last place on earth I wanted to go, but I managed to match his offhand manner and asked, "What kind of hunting?" "Deer. There's a wonderful little place up in the Catskills." Since I hadn't protested by then, he really started to sell. "It's beautiful there; the inn is on a mountain, up in the clouds; the air is cold and dry and full of the smell of the pines; there are miles of trees, all covered with snow."

As I listened to this paean to the hunt, I could imagine only blood and killing and roughneck hunters. I was a city person, predisposed toward the amenities of civilization, and this new adventure horrified me. Still, it seemed awfully important to Bill. So . . . The appointed day came and my misgivings mounted. While I packed some lovely hunting gear I had assembled, Bill seemed to be stowing away a strange mélange of rude impedimenta: heavy woollen longjohns, red railroad handkerchiefs, knitted mittens with one finger, a small baggy pair of coarse red and black britches and an enormous bottle of pine oil. Two automatic shot-guns, checked and rechecked to be sure they were empty, were cased in felt-lined leather scabbards and we were off on a first-light-to-sunset drive north.

The Lake View Inn was a vivid patchwork quilt of hunters' shirts. Outside a blizzard was covering the snow with more snow, and the hunters were clustered around any warmth in the room—the fireplace, the spitting radiators and the bar. The proprietor's wife seemed surprised to find another woman there. The hunters seemed horrified. Still they managed to welcome me and wish me luck with the courtliness and consideration that seems universal in men who hunt.

The sleeping quarters upstairs were untainted by citified con-veniences. Not even heat spoiled their puritan simplicity. The only furniture was two plain metal beds, a washstand and a dresser of ascetic oak. A blurred mirror hung on one wall and a straight length of calico covered the cavern that served as a closet. The only decorations were the frost patterns that formed on the inside of the window and on the ice in the washbasin.

I had originally overlooked a cast iron tub in an alcove of the room, but I will never forget its part in the ritual of the hunt. As I busied myself with unpacking my fetching hunting costumes, Bill seemed to be concocting a witches' brew of scalding water and pine oil. Many of his preparations had seemed peculiar, so I paid this latest activity little attention. But when the alchemy was done, Bill's determined look told me that this was a little different. I was mortified when I realized that the steaming concoction was meant for me. I rebelled at taking off even my sheepskin in that freezing room. But some gentle coaxing quelled my rebellion, and my cloud of Arpège disappeared in a cauldron of essence of pine woods.

The first days of this adventure were full of such rude shocks. The next occurred at 4:45 the following morning—the alarm went off. That jolt was quickly followed by another. My charming hunting gear was pushed deep back into the closet and Bill pro-duced a set of monstrosities for me to wear: red and black woollen britches, longjohns that were pure prickly torment, boots that weighed at least five pounds each.

I took a last look at my beautiful fawn ensemble hanging unused in the closet, and then stepped out into this new phase of my life. With those five-pound boots, every step was an effort, and every step was up. Hills led to mountains and the mountains had more hills on them. And we had to go up all of them—miles and miles up. I had to lift those boots a foot and a half at every step to clear the deep snow.

As the weight of the boots pulled my feet down, the weight of the shotgun pulled me forward, backward or to the side as I tried to find a comfortable way to carry it. The burden seemed much heavier than its six-pound weight. At every new attempt to find a comfortable position, I had to remember not to let the muzzle point anywhere but at the ground. I had to think and check to see that the safety was on. I had to be aware in every cell of my brain that I was carrying a lethal thing. And so I walked, safety on . . . never point in anyone's direction . . . safety on . . . don't let it get caught on barbed wire or twigs . . . safety on . . . safety on . . . safety on—even though the gun was empty. Bill had given me such a long and serious lecture on the dangers and responsibilities of carrying a gun that I would have preferred to forego the shooting part entirely and just go along for the walk.

I was terrified when we got to a clearing and Bill said it was time for me to learn to shoot. He swung an old pail from a tree limb about fifty yards away from me, then walked back and told me to load and fire. I was completely awed by the fact that I was about to discharge the deadly thing.

The first shell snapped up into the chamber, the next two clicked precisely into place. I raised the gun, took off the safety, and shot. The first sound I was aware of after the surprisingly strident bark of the gun (I had expected a mellow boom) was the metallic reverberation of the pail. I shot twice more, and twice more heard the aftersound of a hit as the sound of the gun faded in my hearing. Bill was jubilant. I was relieved that the shooting part seemed to be over. Safety on.

"Good girl! Very good girl! Where did you learn to do that?" I had no idea where I learned. I had simply looked down the metal ramp that runs to the little bead at the end of the gun barrel, and put the little bead on the bucket when I pulled the trigger; other than that I knew absolutely nothing about shooting, except that my hitting the old bucket had somehow made my husband very, very pleased.

"Let's go!" Bill whooped and he actually frolicked into the woods. I think I may have frolicked a bit, too, at least as much as I could while carrying the weight of the boots and gun through the deep snow. "You won't shoot this year," he said, "but you'll do everything else."

That morning "everything else" meant climbing. It seemed that every hill had only an up side. We climbed hills covered with second-growth trees—young, thin trees growing in incredibly dense random patterns. We could see for only fifty yards through their maze. Beyond that the profusion of trunks formed a solid screen. The bare branches made intricate, intersecting patterns on the sky above, black against the bright blue of the sky, the trunks grey in the reflected light of the bright, shadow-thatched blanket of snow. Beyond the second growth we climbed through evergreens. The all-pervading meshing patterns changed to elemental forms: massive conical pines, solid conical shadows, blank, unblemished snow and a hard blue sky. Each pine, each fir, was majestic—and majestically aloof from intrusion on or by its neighbors. Their branches all formed perfect circles at ground level—circles twenty-five feet across—tapering to perfect cones fifty feet above. It was impossible to see more than thirty yards through the trees. Then we climbed beyond the evergreens to pure rock. Jagged crests of granite, steeper than before, almost straight up now, and no trees to grab for help. We climbed and looked and climbed and climbed. And never saw a deer.

I was chagrined. "Do you suppose we got off every trace of my perfume?" I whispered. Bill chuckled quietly and whispered back something I couldn't believe: "Sometimes you don't see a deer all week." I had expected the hunt to be like a battle, with deer behind every tree and hunters shooting from all directions. When Bill had explained that we hunted with shotguns because it was safer and more sporting (they are accurate to only about sixty yards), I had thought that we were using these limited-range guns because of the crowds of people and animals in the woods. But when we stopped to devour our sandwiches and coffee at noon on the first day, I hadn't seen a single deer or person.

In the morning we had hunted the stalk method, actively pursuing the deer. Now I was to learn the "sit." Bill took me to a spot on the edge of a sheer rock gorge, halfway up its quarter-mile length. He made a seat of pine boughs, hung a pair of binoculars around my neck and told me to watch: watch the woods across the gorge, watch the deer crossing down at its end, watch for movement on the hill beyond. Above all, watch deer, their movements, reactions, timing, trails—and what they do when they see me. Bill patted my cap, bussed my cheek and was off to the next ridge line, four miles away. Rendezvous in four hours. I perched on my nest, very alone and not very sure that I should be there. There were two kinds of reality now—the immediate and the panoramic. I found it impossible to think of the ridges I could see forty miles away as being as real as the one I was sitting on. The frigid white stream below was real; the farm beyond the end of the gorge was not. And the bright red back moving away from me was slowly fading into the nether world of vast distance. Bill crossed the top of the next hill and disappeared down its far side, and I was alone.

Alone and still in a vast still world. The air was so cold and dry that I could see a peak seventy miles south perfectly. There was no dirt, no haze. Only the limits of my vision kept me from seeing every needle on every evergreen on it. The clarity was unreal. Behind me a grove of second growth screened my vision off at fifty yards. Across the gully the evergreens filled the mountain full, blocking from sight all but themselves and the cold blue sky. To my left the screen of hardwoods and shield of evergreens came together at the end of the ravine leaving only one clear patch, like a keyhole through the trees, where the stream cut through. But on my right the gully widened out to open on empty hills dotted with pine or oak rolling in seemingly endless massive waves of earth.

A small mechanical toy appeared on the face of the second line of hills. The vivid red coat inching up through the snow commanded recognition over the mile of empty air between us. Bill was perfectly visible through the crystalline air, but the distance and the unreal slowness of his movements through the encumbering snow made him seem like a figure in a soft-focus, slow-motion film. He stooped under a barbed wire fence as if in a distant dream. A grove of birch made white line patterns over the red jacket against the snow as he slipped through their maze. A stand of pine or a hill obscured the scarlet patch as it moved away, but even two miles out the color and motion drew my eye as soon as Bill was beyond the obstruction.

Now another object penetrated my consciousness through the stillness and the loneliness. A dog—two ridges away—patrolling the pastures of a farm. Bill, two miles out, was unreal. The farmer, on the ridge beyond, was a toy. But the dog was real, his faraway, slow-motion unreality contradicted by the forceful assertion of his bark, quietly, but clearly, audible. Leaping and shaking his head, he looked like a miniature animal in a Christmas crèche, but a second and a half later the arrival of the faint sound of him affirmed his reality.

Quite suddenly I was aware of the sharp sting of incredible cold in my toes and fingers. A bone-deep cold that had been only crisp-chill in the morning's leg-aching exertion now numbed me. Two hours had drifted by in time that seemed no time at all. My absorption in the vast unreality of the mountains had compressed the period of my fascination into an instant of unreal time.

My limbs were stiff, but I managed to get off one glove and touched a wooden hand to my wooden face. Neither cheeks nor fingers felt the touch. For an instant I didn't know why I was there or what I was doing. I only felt the cold of the air and the cold of my hands and face and feet and knew that I must find warmth. I jumped and beat my hands and shuffled my feet, and then was jolted by a patch of red emerging above the tree line on a mountain four miles away. It was Bill, and I remembered that I had to endure two more hours of this cold before he would be back.

I was desperate and horrified. I fumbled in my pocket for two precious bits of contraband from my former life—a lipstick and a mirror—but they only added to the horror. When I looked into the mirror I saw that my face was actually distorted by the cold—swollen, chapped, with a subtle trace of blue. First I despaired, then raged. How did Bill dare do this to me? What had possessed him? Why would he leave me here in the unmoving mass of sub-zero air to freeze?

My rage turned into rebellion, and the rebellion turned to heat

Hills led to
mountains and
the mountains
had more hills
on them.
And
we had
to go up
all of them—
miles and
miles up.

Venison is a powerful meal—on our palates and our emotions.

within me. I found the energy and agility to sweep the pine boughs
off my perch and scrawl a defiant GONE BACK TO LODGE on the rock
with my lipstick. Then I remembered that I didn't know how to
get back to the lodge.

I stayed, and swore that I'd never come again, and moved and
flapped my arms and rubbed my hands to keep warm even though
it probably meant that every deer in the county knew exactly where
I was. I stomped and fumed—body heat was no problem now.
And I looked at the scenery. But now I looked at individual parts
instead of drenching my sight with the entire panorama. The dog
on the farm two ridges away was out and barking, protecting
a peace that probably hadn't been disturbed since the British in-
fantry marched through during the Revolutionary War.

Then the red spot on the barn was matched by a red dot cresting
the nearer ridge. Bill was almost back! I felt as if I was about to
be rescued from the Arctic, forgetting for a moment that it was
my rescuer who had marooned me. As soon as he was within shouting distance I yelled that I was coming down to meet him and
scrambled down the rock face. Boulders and branches gave steadying handholds until I got to the gentler slope of the hill, then I
broke into a gallop to Bill's side.

Dusk was falling, the end of the day's hunting, no need for quiet
now. Our chatter and laughter streamed behind us as we walked
down to the road. "What did you write on the rock?" Bill asked.
I was dumbfounded. Then I remembered his binoculars, and the
fury that was dispelled by my rescue returned. How dare he read
my message, even if it was meant for him? But he swore that he
was just scanning for deer and had seen the scarlet against the
grey rock, but couldn't decipher the words.

In other, more civilized, times I had dined in many of the world's
finest restaurants, but never with the gusto I lavished on the plain
home-cooked food that was heaped on my plate that night. The
rustic bed, piled high with quilts, gave me the luxurious and re-
newing sleep of total exhaustion. And at dawn we were out again.
And the next dawn. And the next. And we stayed out till dusk
every time.

For three more days I climbed through hardwood and pine, I
climbed over shale and up rock quarry sides. I climbed until my

legs were too tired even to ache. And I sat—countless, endless frozen hours of sitting and watching. Every experience was re-experienced dozens of times. Every climb was a repetition of an earlier climb. Every wait seemed to be an extension of that first interminable wait, as if my rescue had never come and I had always sat and watched and would always do so. And every night I ate a meal for a giant and slept the deep sleep of unconsciousness. The experiences were the same, but with slight differences. Each day brought more awareness, more understanding of what we were about. We had still seen no deer, but we had seen signs of them. I learned the subtle differences between deer tracks a day and an hour old. I started noticing bark scraped off trees at antler height that meant a buck had polished and sharpened his rack there.

A still steaming pile of pellets led to a half-day stalk. We followed the trail, scouting ahead, followed again. We tracked through thickets and pine growth, across fields and gullies. An area of bare rock meant no trail, and a careful scouting of the rock's periphery to find where the deer had left it. For five hours the buck eluded us. His tracks said he must weigh two hundred pounds and carry at least an eight-point rack, but except for those tracks he might have been a ghost. The tracks and the day ended in a thick cordon of pine and we were back to the lodge again.

By the fourth night I'd seen and learned enough to be impressed by the finesse of the hunter. How did Bill walk through the snow without a sound, when it creaked so under my boots, though I am only half his weight? How did he, half again my size, avoid branches that tangled me?

I learned to look for the small signs that hint at a deer nearby. The sassing of a bluejay—it might be for us or for a buck. A metallic flash that could be an antler. A branch that moves horizontally, the flick of white of a retreating rump, a curled-up form on a sunny ledge, all could be deer.

I began to be aware of many small things in the forest that I had never noticed in casual walks in the woods, different and distinct sounds that had been undifferentiated noise before. The creaking of the trees in the cold. The staccato rap of the woodpecker. The startling whirr of a flushed partridge. The rattle of squirrels leaping from branch to branch, and their chatter on seeing us—or have they seen a deer? Even if they had, by the end of the fourth day we had not.

On the fifth day, just as I was beginning to feel that I knew the terrain of the area we were hunting, Bill decided to switch to the next county. We got out extra early, and just before dawn we took up our stands on one of a pair of near mirror-image hills facing each other across a valley.

The common element of the twin hills was a dirt road bisecting the valley between them. On either side of the road, clearings sloped gently upward—the one on our side bare, the opposite one dotted with worn-out apple trees. At the high ends of the clearings were stone walls, and beyond them thick pines rolled up to the craggy stone of the mountain tops. A narrow fringe of trees ran down to the road from the center of the wall behind which we sat. On the opposite side it was matched by a hedgerow that ran up to the pines.

We picked positions about three hundred yards apart beside the stone wall and settled in to wait. We scanned the opposite ridge— first the bald spot near the top, then the edge of the pines, and finally the hedgerow. Occasionally we would glance over the clearing, but if the deer were going to come, they would avoid the open ground and stay close to cover. We checked the woods behind us, and looked along the wall from time to time, on the chance of seeing a deer which had seen us and "frozen." Bill had picked the spot, as he had picked all of our previous spots, because it was a deer thoroughfare. Deer like to move in cover, and the line of trees and the line of hedgerow provided one of the few grown-over routes between the mountain on which we sat and the ridge-line across the valley.

And so we sat. Concealed and quiet—not moving, for the slightest movement would alert the deer. Not making a sound that their incredibly sensitive ears would hear as danger. And we watched. I saw Bill move before I saw the deer. I glanced down along the wall more for the comforting reassurance that he was there than in the expectation of seeing a deer (which I now suspected might exist only in hunters' imaginations), and saw him creeping along, crouched down behind the wall, toward the line of trees. I remembered his warning against sudden movements, and turned my head slowly toward the opposite hill. At first I saw nothing. The hill was exactly as it had been for the previous two hours—a stage set for action but with no players. Then a shadow in the hedgerow moved. And I saw that it wasn't a shadow, but a shape. I knew that it must be a deer, but could not yet see it clearly. Then another shadow inched forward and I began to be able to see the members of the small herd moving toward us. The shapes had hop-scotched halfway down the hedgerow and I had yet to see one clearly when they bolted. Five deer—three does, a fawn and a buck—exploded out of the camouflage of the dappled shadows and raced down the hill, across the road and halfway up our hill, parallel to the tree line. About fifty yards downhill from the spot in the trees where Bill was hiding they angled away from the cover. The scent of man had alerted them to the danger, but they weren't sure where it was. They covered fifty more yards uphill in seconds, bounding fifteen feet at each leap. Then two sharp explosions scattered them in a wild, graceful flight to the tree line. It took a second (the deer were now twenty yards closer to safety) for me to realize that Bill had shot, yet all five were running. Another second of wondering why he had not shot again and they were to the wall. Then as the does and fawn vanished into the pines, the buck dropped. There was no sign that he had been hit—no slowing, no stumbling—just frantic flight, then absolute stillness. It was as if the sound of the shot had started him running, but the slugs had not struck home till five leaps later.

I checked the safety of my gun and started out toward Bill. By the time I had reached him he had dragged the deer to a tree and was hoisting him up onto a limb by a rope tied to his antlers. As soon as the deer was up and the rope secured to hold him, Bill slit him down the middle from breastbone to tail.

I was prepared to faint or be sick, but my reaction surprised me. Instead of revulsion at the sight of the newly dead animal being butchered, I felt a very basic satisfaction. The animal was beautiful and surprisingly fragile, and it was sobering to see it as an inanimate thing when just minutes ago I had watched it leap up the hill to preserve the life within itself. But beyond the appreciation of its beauty and vitality, and the regret that they no longer existed, was the awareness that it was food. I had the strange and startling realization that all my life I had been eating the flesh of animals killed and butchered by others for my convenience. It was good, it felt very right and very fitting to be there harvesting part of my sustenance for myself. The entire concept of eating took on far greater significance then, with the understanding that life is sustained by the elimination of other life. It seems a simple thing—something everyone knows rationally. But I had never had the appreciation of the endless cycle of deaths that are necessary for life until I participated in the hunt.

After slitting the deer, Bill cut off the genitalia and opened the carcass to let the viscera drop out, then he reached up into the chest cavity, cut the esophagus and pulled out the heart and lungs. The heart had been pierced by one of the slugs and was demolished, but the liver was intact, so we wrapped it in a plastic bag to have fried fresh that night. When he had cut away the flesh around the slugs' entrance and exit wounds, Bill propped the field-dressed carcass open with a sharp stick and sat down for a cigarette. The steam of the still warm organs in the snow and the smoke of the cigarette made clouds—one of victory, one of defeat, both signifying the end of the contest.

After the deer had drained for half an hour we covered the carcass with cheesecloth, lowered it and pulled it to the road. I waited with our catch while Bill started out for the car, about a mile away. Back at the inn we hung the deer in a shed and our hunt was over.

Most hunters take their deer to a butcher for cutting up, but Bill prefers to do our own. After the deer has hung a week it is skinned. Bill continues the slit used to gut the animal well up into the neck (unless the buck is a trophy), then cuts around the neck and pulls the skin down, peeling the carcass. The legs are cut off at the knee to avoid the danger of being cut by the sharp hooves during the skinning. The skin of each leg is slit from the knee into the center slit so they can be stripped with the torso.

When the carcass has been completely skinned we cut it in half just behind the rib cage for easier handling. We cut loins into roasts and into individual steaks. The ribs are cut into chops, two ribs to a chop; the shoulders become pot roasts; the neck, brisket and one rump are cut into stew chunks and are ground for venison burgers and venison chili. One haunch is reserved for Roasted

Haunch of Venison. All cuts, even those to be ground, must be trimmed of all fat, since venison fat, unlike that of domestic animals, has an unpleasant taste and gristly texture.

After butchering and trimming, all cuts are marinated in Basic Game Marinade for five days in covered crocks kept in a cool place. Like most game, deer can be frozen after being marinated. Venison feasts are always the most hearty and satisfying of the winter. We serve venison with Purée of Chestnuts and Wild Cherry Jelly, pungent, earthy tastes that reinforce the heady, heavy taste of the venison itself. A robust Burgundy adds its own strong yet blending note to the meal, and we finish, as we finish all of our game feasts, with Wild Cherry Liqueur.

The venison is a powerful meal—on our palates and our emotions. The vigorous flavors of the meat recall the vigorous pursuit of the game. The robust tastes and memories mingle and blend into a sensation of deep, basic satisfaction with our catch and with ourselves—a sensation that can only be had through the entire, primeval experience of the catch and the feast.

Feasting on Venison

Venison must hang for a period of 7 days to 4 weeks. All cuts of venison must be marinated for 5 days in Basic Game Marinade.

Basic Game Marinade

For each ten pounds of venison.

Salt
Freshly ground black pepper
4 onions, sliced
3 carrots, sliced
4 cloves
8 peppercorns, crushed
3 bay leaves
3 garlic cloves, pressed
6 sprigs parsley
4 juniper berries
6 cups red wine
2 cups olive oil
2 cups vinegar

Season venison with salt and pepper. Place in earthenware or stone crock and cover with layers of vegetables and spices. Mix together the wine, olive oil and vinegar and pour over meat. Cover crock, place in very cool area or in refrigerator for 5 days. Turn meat each day. If stored in refrigerator, take crock out daily and allow to stand for 2 hours at room temperature.

After 5 days remove meat and pat dry with cloth. Reserve marinade for cooking and sauces.

Roast Haunch of Venison

Feast for 14

Haunch of venison
Salt pork
¼ cup butter
4 tablespoons olive oil
1 cup reserved marinade
6 strips bacon
2 tablespoons each butter and potato flour
1 glass red wine
4 tablespoons Wild Cherry Jelly

After five days in Basic Game Marinade, remove venison haunch and pat dry. Lard with strips of salt pork.

Combine butter and olive oil in large, heavy skillet and brown haunch gently on all sides.

Boil down reserved marinade to half original volume and strain over venison.

Lay bacon strips over venison and roast in moderate oven (350 degrees) for four hours, basting frequently. When venison is tender, remove to heated platter and keep warm.

Reduce pan sauces by cooking down.

Add butter, flour, wine and Wild Cherry Jelly and blend well with pan drippings.

Strain over venison.

Serve with Purée of Chestnuts, glazed white onions and wild rice.

Venison Chasseur

Feast for 16

10 pounds venison, cubed
¼ pound butter
6 tablespoons olive oil
⅓ cup hot sherry
5 pounds pearl onions
3 pounds large fresh white mushrooms
3 tablespoons tomato paste

13

2 shallots, chopped
1 clove garlic, pressed
2½ tablespoons meat glaze
5 tablespoons potato flour
4 cups beef stock
4 cups red wine
Salt
Freshly ground pepper
8 sprigs parsley
4 sprigs thyme
4 sprigs tarragon
6 shoots chive
Chopped fresh parsley

Cut rump of venison into large cubes and brown in hot butter and olive oil. Pour hot sherry over venison, and remove venison to heated bowl.

Brown onions in the pan, add mushrooms and cook until golden brown, then remove onions and mushrooms to warmed bowl holding venison.

14 Add tomato paste, garlic, shallots, meat glaze and potato flour to pan and stir until smooth. Add stock and bring to boil. Add two cups of the red wine. Season. Add venison, and bouquet of parsley, thyme, tarragon and chives tied in cheesecloth bag.

Cover and simmer very slowly for 1½ hours.

Add onions and mushrooms and one cup red wine.

Continue simmering for 45 minutes longer, adding the remaining red wine as required.

Sprinkle with chopped parsley.

Serve with Wild Cherry Jelly and wild rice.

Venison Steak

Feast for 4—Eastern European Style

4 venison steaks
¼ cup butter
½ cup reserved marinade
1 cup sour cream
Salt
Freshly ground black pepper

Cut loin of venison into 1½-inch steaks.

Melt butter in large skillet; when it froths, sear steaks on both sides to desired doneness.

Remove venison to heated platter.

Add reserved marinade and bring to boil.

Spoon out some of the boiling mixture into bowl, add the sour cream and a pinch of salt. Blend. (This will keep the cream from curdling when introduced into the skillet.)

Add cream to simmering marinade and allow to simmer gently for 2 minutes. Season. Serve over steaks.

Venison Chili

Feast for 6

2 cups red kidney beans
¼ pound white salt pork, diced
2 fresh green peppers, diced
2 medium onions, diced
3 pounds ground venison
4 tablespoons chili powder
2 tablespoons tomato paste
2 cans tomato soup
1 cup beef stock
Salt
Freshly ground pepper

Soak kidney beans overnight, then boil for 30 minutes with ½ teaspoon soda.

Slowly try diced salt pork in heavy skillet.

Add diced green peppers and onions. Sauté until transparent golden color.

Add ground venison and stir with wooden spoon until delicately browned.

Blend in chili powder, tomato paste, tomato soup and beef stock. Cover. Simmer for 1¼ hours.

Fold in kidney beans.

Season. Continue simmering for 20 minutes.

Serve with crisp salted crackers.

Venison Burgers de Luxe

1 teaspoon red wine
½ pound ground venison per person
¼ teaspoon marjoram
¼ teaspoon thyme
¼ teaspoon tarragon
Salt
Freshly ground pepper
Chopped fresh parsley

Blend wine into chopped venison and form into oblong loaves, allowing ½ pound for each loaf.

Sprinkle over with marjoram, thyme, tarragon, salt and pepper.
Keep at room temperature for ½ hour.
Sear in hot butter; serve very rare.
Serve with Venison Sauce.

Venison Sauce

1 pound mushrooms, sliced
½ cup butter
2 shallots, chopped
1 cup red wine
Salt
Freshly ground black pepper
1 cup brown sauce
1 tablespoon tomato paste
½ teaspoon each chopped parsley, tarragon, thyme

Wash and dry mushrooms.
Slice thinly and sauté lightly in frothing butter, using wooden
spoon to turn.
Add shallots and wine, salt and pepper and cook until mixture
is reduced by half.
Add brown sauce, tomato paste, parsley, tarragon and thyme.
Serve hot.

Purée of Chestnuts

2 pounds French or Italian chestnuts
⅓ cup chicken stock
2 tablespoons butter
2 tablespoons Wild Cherry Jelly
Salt
Freshly ground black pepper

Cook chestnuts in boiling water until tender. Drain.
Make crisscross slits in the flat side while still hot and peel off
shells.
Rub chestnuts through sieve or put into blender.
Add chicken stock, butter, Wild Cherry Jelly, salt and pepper,
and mix thoroughly.

16

Chapter 2.

The Wild Goose Hunt

All the thrill of the goose hunt is distilled into an hour-long vigil to sunset. We stand motionless in a blind of tall reeds, eyes constantly scanning the sky arc by arc. There are no geese there yet, but we cannot move. Long before they are close enough for us to see them, the geese could see the slightest motion we might make. And so we peer—eyes straining to turn, lift, scan, heads absolutely still—as the sky goes from grey to violet.

We keep our chins down and our parkas up, to show as little face as possible to the sky. The doubts begin to stir. "Will they come?" "Are the decoys true?" "Did we leave a telltale scrap of paper?"

They've been here every dusk we've checked, but the flight might have migrated farther south today. Will they come? Will they come? We scan left, center, right. Up right, up center, up left. At the end of each sweep muscles strain to move a fraction more. There is profound stillness. No word has passed between us since the stand began. The only sound is the wind's steady chaffing of reeds, but a strange communication has begun. We share a complete consciousness of each other's mind and nerves. There can be only one thought: "Will they come?" There is only one feeling: an all-pervading tingling of excitement.

Still we ache, motionless, and still we scan. Eyes left, center—

when the first sound comes. It is a faint, almost imperceptible honking, and we are transformed. Our eyes find another bit of strength to strain even farther out, but still no goose is in sight. Excitement sparks back and forth between us.

Another honk, much louder now, and then a chorus—and suddenly they burst into sight, a mile out and a quarter mile high! We strain at perfect stillness as they bank down into their descent. We can guess now—maybe two dozen. Half a mile now, and coming incredibly fast—their honking is almost a solid sound. Their four-foot wings are spread and set. They glide like massive projectiles, straight and fast.

At a quarter mile we pick our shots. They keep coming. Fast, lower. Gun up, safety off, shoot! One! Got him! Shoot—another! The blasts and the geese fill our minds with an explosion of noise and action.

Then the honkers are gone. We click on our safeties and leap out of our blind to retrieve our catch. There's one—another, two more —that's it! The limit!

We break into a delicious soul-filling laugh. The catch—our catch! We did it!

There's no effort imaginable that wouldn't be worth making for that moment, but we actually enjoyed it with very little effort at all. An old traditional goose hunt is a day-long ordeal for men only—an unendurably cold pre-dawn watch in a clammy pit, a day of endless and uncomfortable waiting, bone-chilled exhaustion at sunset. And all of it unnecessary.

We've condensed the sensations of the hunt into one superb afternoon, and eliminated almost all of the discomforts. Instead of waiting in a hole and hoping for the geese to come to us, we go to wherever the geese happen to be. Our portable blind saves us hours of discomfort while hunting, and eliminates days of drudgery that go into digging a conventional goose stand.

Making the portable blind is a lazy morning job. All it takes is four lengths of army surplus webbing, an old tarpaulin, four straight two-inch hardwood branches about six feet long, four twelve-foot lengths of rope and a half-dozen fat armfuls of cattails. Bill trims the twigs off the branches and sharpens one end of each to a point to make stakes, while I spread out the webbing and weave the cattails through the holes in thick clumps. About twelve stalks of cattails go into each row with their tops at random lengths between ten inches and a foot and a half above the top of the lattice to give the blind an irregular, natural look.

When the webbing has been stuffed with as many cattails as it can hold, we roll it around the stakes and add an armful of extra reeds for final touches and repairs. Next, the tarpaulin goes around the rolled-up blind. We tie the whole bundle together with the ropes, and we're set.

Whether we're hunting on James Bay or Long Island, we wear our ritual goose hunting outfits. I have a baby sealskin parka, pants and mucklucks and Bill sports a more conventional (and incredibly ancient) combination of canvas trousers, parka and boots.

Although our costumes are literally poles apart in appearance, they have several basics in common. First, they are warm. Even though we're not in the field for long, we stand absolutely motionless for at least an hour, and that hour is the coldest one of a cold afternoon. Our parkas and sweaters do not bind or restrain us in any way, since we have to move fast and smoothly when the geese come in. The fields are damp so our boots are waterproof. Finally, everything we wear is in flat, subdued earth colors.

T he guns we prefer for Canada goose are 12-gauge pump guns with 30-inch barrels, but the type of gun is not as important as the fit. A gun must come to your shoulder easily and feel comfortable while up. Since geese are usually shot at longer range than most shotgun game, long barrels and full chokes are helpful. We usually use No. 2 magnum shells for honkers. This load has the tighter pattern and extra pellets needed for big fowl at long distances, although a smaller No. 4 or No. 6 duck load can also be used.

Despite their almost incredible perception of color and motion in the blind, geese are fairly easily fooled by decoys. Everything from clumps of weeds to diapers has been used with success. The ones we use are just silhouettes cut out of plywood or masonite and attached to stakes. We make them much larger than life size for extra visibility, and hinge the necks so they can be arranged in natural feeding positions. Bill bought one decoy at an antique shop near where we hunt to establish a profile and color pattern, and then we made a flock of our own. Between ten and twenty decoys are enough to bring in a flight. A goose call, and our gear is complete.

We pick our hunting field on afternoon and evening drives a few weeks before the start of the season, scouting the local farms and fields around dusk to see where the geese are feeding. Although all hunting stops at sundown, it doesn't matter if you check the fields later—if the geese are there, they probably came before dark. We check a promising field several times to be sure it's a regular stopping place.

Geese usually spend the night where they can find food. Harvested grain fields or wild strawberry patches are ideal, but you have to look carefully. A field that seems barren at first glance might offer a feast to a goose. I would have passed up dozens of fields if Bill hadn't shown me how to look for tiny bits of grain and seeds that are left on the ground for as long as a year after the field's crops have been harvested.

Discovering a good field is only half of what it takes to get to hunt it. Almost invariably, the best spots are posted—surrounded by "no hunting" signs. The interesting part of getting a field is convincing the owner that those signs shouldn't apply to you. Our approach varies from farmer to farmer, but a bottle of good bourbon is the universally accepted token of appreciation when we're given permission to hunt. Later, when the hunt is successfully over, we always give the owner one of the geese.

The hunt begins about two hours before sunset when we arrive at the field to set up the blind. Geese land into the wind, and toward the decoys, so we erect the blind a little upwind of the decoys and about twenty-five feet to the side of the end of the glide path.

We form the blind by driving the stakes into the ground in an irregular pattern and stringing the reed-filled webbing between them, tapering it in toward the top. The spare cattails are used to patch corners or any bare spots, and the tarpaulin forms a floor. The blind resembles a haystack or pile of cornstalks when it's finished.

Next we put out the decoys. They must all face into the wind and keep grouped into a flock. We set their heads into various feeding positions and arrange them so they cast realistic shadows, which are as visible and as important as the decoys themselves. That's it. We move our car a few hundred feet down the road, check for anything we might have left lying out to alert the geese, smooth our footprints around the decoys and enter the blind. Last cigarette, safety on, load guns, find a comfortable position and take our stand.

The sun will be up for just an hour more, and before it sets the geese must come. They may be coming now, so we must not move, we can only watch—searching every piece of upwind sky for a trace. And finally we hear them call.

Keeping our guns down and keeping still as the geese come streaking in is the hardest part of the hunt. At a quarter mile out we pick our shots—then watch and wait.

Ten excruciating seconds—and each second means twenty-five yards. Up two seconds early and they'll still be out of range. Wait, wait, wait—until my bird is in my line of fire. Until Bill has a target, too. Then up! Safety off and swing onto a six-foot lead. Shoot! One careful shot at a time. The bird drops. Swing onto another. Lead up as he climbs. Shoot! Wing shot . . . less lead as he falters. Shoot! And he drops! I heard Bill's gun blast only twice—that means two hits. Two geese are the limit. A miss would mean another shot. Safety on, and we charge out to our geese. We pack up the blind, pick up the decoys, drop a goose off at the farmer's house. The hunt is finished.

The geese must be dressed out immediately after the hunt. To begin, we make a four-inch slit from the base of each spine toward the front of the carcass. Then we reach in carefully, to avoid enlarging the slits, and pull out all entrails. We save the livers for Wild Goose Liver Pâté. A good fistful of salt goes into each bird and we shake it vigorously to coat the entire cavity.

Next, Bill loops a leather thong around each bird's neck and hangs it under the eaves on the north side of the house. The geese must be hung in a spot that is shaded all day, and where the air can circulate freely around them. A cool barn, an unheated room, and the top shelf of a refrigerator with lower shelves removed are all good spots. The temperature during the hanging period should not be allowed to exceed 36 degrees at any time. After five days of aging, the geese must be plucked. Reluctance to face up to this once arduous job probably accounts for many of the "hung-until-their-necks-drop-off" theories that have frightened off so many would-be game enthusiasts.

Old-fashioned plucking was agony. White down was everywhere —in nostrils, hair, eyebrows, eyelashes—the fluff coating the room with tickling irritation. Fortunately there's a way to avoid the misery (and most of the work) that plucking used to entail.

When our geese are ready for plucking we clip off their wings just beyond the joint (leaving enough of the joint so that no cavity is created), then dip each bird into a cast iron kettle filled with four pounds of melted paraffin, making sure that the goose is completely coated. Next we hang it outdoors for approximately ten minutes. When the wax has hardened we rip it off with abrupt yanks down long narrow strips. When all of the wax is gone, so are the feathers and down. Even if stubborn pinfeathers should be left a repeat of the waxing and stripping will leave the bird completely smooth and feather-free.

The very soul of any game meal is the marinade. It anoints the wild flesh with an exquisite and subtle contrapuntal piquancy. To begin, we arrange layers of finely sliced carrots, sliced onions, sprigs of parsley, bay leaves, peppercorns, crushed garlic, cloves and juniper berries on the bottom of an earthen crock about fourteen inches in diameter. The goose is placed on top of this bed and is covered with repeated layers of the same condiments. We combine a bottle and a half of good red Bordeaux with tarragon vinegar, olive oil and a few pinches of salt, and pour the concoction over the goose. The crock must be covered with an earthen lid and stored in a cool (but not freezing) place. We turn the bird from time to time to be sure that every part is completely immersed. The bird is removed after three to five days and patted dry with cheesecloth. It's now ready for feast or freezer.

We like to prepare the Wild Cherry and Chestnut Dressing at least one day in advance of the feast. It requires a good bit of effort, but is well worth every minute and every ingredient expended.

The goose should be stuffed plumply, but care must be taken to avoid any overflow.

*Instead of
waiting in a
hole and hoping
for the geese
to come to us,
we go to
wherever the
geese happen
to be.*

The geese must be hung in a spot that is shaded all day, and where air can circulate freely around them.

Because a Canada goose is a wild flying thing, it has none of the fat of domestic birds. It must be generously larded and continuously basted while roasting. The best way to do this is to dot it with butter chunks and wrap it with salt pork slices and long fatty bacon strips. There should be several butter chunks under each strip of bacon, and the bacon should completely encase the bird. This will provide enough fat for the slow, continuous basting that is the secret of tender wild goose. A ten-pound Canada goose requires four hours of roasting in a 350-degree oven. For the final hour, we remove the roasting pan lid and bacon strips and baste the bird with pan drippings every ten minutes.

The goose feast begins with an exotic and appropriate appetizer: Wild Goose Liver Pâté. Then we bring on the goose. Served with Wild Cherry and Chestnut Dressing, Purée of Chestnuts, and a field salad, it is an exquisite symphony of rich, complementary flavors and delicately contrasting dissonances. A hearty but not heavy Bordeaux makes delineations and transitions between the heady flavors. Add espresso and dry Wild Cherry Liqueur for dessert and the wild goose feast is over.

Feasting on Wild Goose

Geese must be dressed immediately after the hunt, and hung for 5 days before plucking. They should then be marinated for 3 to 5 days in Basic Game Marinade, using same quantities as for 10 pounds of venison.

Roast Canada Goose

10-pound Canada goose (hung and marinated)
½ lemon
2 tablespoons brandy
Wild Cherry and Chestnut Dressing
½ pound butter
½ pound sliced salt pork
½ pound sliced bacon

Preheat oven to 400 degrees.
Rub goose inside and out with cut lemon and brandy.
Stuff with Wild Cherry and Chestnut Dressing. Skewer and truss the bird.
Dot goose with dollops of softened butter.

Place salt pork slices over breast.

Wrap bacon slices all around goose "mummy" fashion, encasing butter chunks and salt pork slices.

Put into oven in covered roasting pan.

After 20 minutes, reduce heat to 350 degrees.

After 3 hours remove bacon and pork wrappings.

Roast uncovered for 1 hour longer, basting every 10 minutes.

Serve with Purée of Chestnuts and Wild Cherry Jelly.

Wild Cherry and Chestnut Dressing

4 tablespoons bacon drippings
½ cup each chopped onions, chopped celery, sliced fresh mushrooms
1 pound homemade pork sausage
1 clove garlic, pressed
1 teaspoon rosemary
½ teaspoon thyme
¼ teaspoon sage
1 bay leaf
Salt
Freshly ground black pepper
1 goose liver, chopped
3 tart cooking apples, diced
1 cup diced day-old bread
2 tablespoons chopped parsley
3 tablespoons Wild Cherry Jelly
1 pound cooked chestnuts, coarsely chopped
1 cup chicken stock
1 cup dry white wine

24

Heat bacon drippings in large heavy skillet and sauté onion, celery and mushrooms gently.

Stir in sausage with wooden spoon.

Add garlic, rosemary, thyme, sage, bay leaf, salt and pepper.

Cook until sausage is lightly browned all over.

Remove excess fat.

Add goose liver and cook for 2 minutes, stirring carefully.

Remove from heat, blend in apples, bread, parsley, jelly, chestnuts, chicken stock and wine. Cool.

Refrigerate overnight. Bring to room temperature at least 2 hours before stuffing goose.

Wild Goose Liver Pâté

4 wild Canada goose livers
¼ cup rendered chicken fat
¼ cup butter
2 tablespoons finely minced onions

¾ teaspoon dry mustard
1 teaspoon salt
⅛ teaspoon ground cloves
Pinch of nutmeg
Freshly ground black pepper
1 tablespoon cognac
6 truffles, sliced

Cover livers with water and bring to boil. Simmer for 20 minutes in covered saucepan.

Drain and put livers through sieve.

Mix liver paste with chicken fat, butter, onions and spices.

Blend in cognac and truffles.

Pack into small earthen or stone crock and chill.

25

Chapter 3.

Pheasant: Elegant Feast and Feathers

The pheasant hunt is a ceremony. Every motion, every method has had generations of faithful observation and practice. And, since the traditional way is so pleasant and so effective, this is one hunt on which we follow the old customs to the letter.

Since pheasant is usually the first hunt of the year, our ritual begins with hand trap shooting the day before the hunt itself. We are always chagrined at how badly our aim has deteriorated during the spring and summer, but an afternoon's shooting is usually enough to put us back on form.

This year, however, it was going to be especially difficult. Shotguns for pheasant are generally bored (or choked) for a fairly wide pattern of shot if single-barreled, and bored with one wide and one tight patterned barrel if double-barreled. A wide pattern is preferred for the first shot of double-barrel (and over and under) guns, and for all shots of single-barrel guns (pump or automatic) because most shots at pheasant are from fairly close range, and the smaller shot pattern of a tight choke makes hitting them nearly impossible. The difficulty this year was that Bill decided that we were going to hunt with full choke guns.

"It's more sporting," he said when I protested. "And besides, with full choke guns we can concentrate on head shots and not have all those pellets in the meat." I rebelled. Pheasant is one of my favorite game foods, and I envisioned a scoreless hunt. But my tantrum and my dire prophecy of a fall without Pheasant in Cream Sauce might just as well have been sweet compliance for all the effect they had on Bill. Finally he said, "Well, *I* can connect with a full choke gun. If you don't think you can, maybe you should use improved cylinder." I twisted the polychoke on my favorite old Remington to extra full choke, and we were off for clay target shooting.

It was a cold, colorless fall day. The grey sky and drizzling mist masked the changing leaves of the trees around the field where we shoot. The dull yellow leaves and the drab yellow grass made a bleak, muddied duotone out of the otherwise all grey landscape. It was cold enough to merit gloves, the shooting difficult enough to prohibit them.

We took a box of clay pigeons and a hand trap for throwing them, along with my shotgun and a half dozen boxes of shells. Since Bill was using a 12-gauge gun and I was using a 20-gauge, we left his gun and shells behind to minimize the chance of a dangerous mix-up of gun and shell gauges.

I loaded my automatic, and my humiliation began. I brought the gun up as I heard Bill say "Ready" from somewhere behind me. I called out "Pull" and a yellow and black disk soared out and up against the grey sky. I looked, swung the gun and shot—three fast, deadly accurate shots—and the disk soared on, then down to an unscathed landing. I reloaded quickly, determined to powder the next target. The disk flew lower this time, in a flat, fast trajectory. I waited. Bead on the target. Lead just enough. Check the lead. And then it was too late to shoot. I heard "Ready" and yelled back "Pull" reflexively. The pigeon was high and to my right. I swung on and fired, and it exploded into shreds at the sound of the blast. Finally. I called out "Pull!" again, and regressed with two clean misses.

Bill stopped throwing and came up to offer some advice. "You're not leading enough. Remember, the target is moving fast. Don't swing up on the pigeon, follow its path and swing onto it and past it in one smooth sweep. And keep swinging as you shoot. Follow through, or you'll be shooting late."

I concentrated on the flying disks, the gold bead on the end of the gun barrel and the crucial arc of air that had to separate the two when I pulled the trigger. "Ready." "Pull!" And then the blasts. The next hour was a steady rhythm of the sounds repeated and repeated again, punctuated by the clicks of the shells going into the magazine. By the time my arms were trembling tired, and my shoulder was slightly numb and sore from the kick, I was powdering a pigeon with almost every shot.

We put away my gun and the few 20-gauge shells that were left and I began to throw for Bill. With nothing to do but put the clay pigeons in the hand trap and fling them out, I could watch their arc against the flat grey sky in their graceful elliptical flights. But soon Bill was interrupting those flights with enough regularity so that we could go home, confident of a good bag the next day.

It was first light and foggy when we got to the preserve, but by the time we had checked in and had some coffee the day had broken clear and bright. We met our guide and went out to pick a dog. At the kennel area we were greeted by pandemonium. Every dog competed with every other dog in trying to bark loudest and jump highest to command our attention and be picked to accompany us. The guide suggested one of the setters, and turned her loose. She was so excited at the prospect of a hunt that when we stopped to talk for a minute before setting out, she took the guide's hand in her mouth and began leading him into the field. We were amazed to find that this frolicking puppy was actually thirteen years old. Her daily hunting had given her the spirit, stamina and appearance of a dog a quarter her age. Her eyes glistened in anticipation of doing her work as she frisked ahead, practicing flushing birds from the bushes on the way to the fields.

The morning mist had left the leaves and grasses wet, so the pheasant would be reluctant to fly, but whether or not the birds were ready, the dog was, so we obliged her and started our hunt. The first field was about five acres of wild grass, sparse and yellow, bordered by bright-pink-leaved dogwoods against a deep-green pine background. I didn't think that there could be any pheasant in the field, for the cover was so sparse we would have seen them, but almost as soon as the dog started to hunt she was standing immobile, nose pointed, tail straight out.

The first shot was to be mine, so I walked up to about twenty feet

29

behind her position. The guide went up to the dog, took her off point and sent her into the grass to flush the bird. She scurried about for a while with no luck, so he joined her in beating the bushes.

The bird exploded straight up into the air, directly above the dog and guide. "Shoot," he called, but I was petrified. I had always been taught never to point even an empty gun in the general direction of anything I didn't want to shoot, and now the guide was shouting for me to fire at a target only ten feet over his head. I couldn't and wouldn't shoot while the bird was so close to him, but after its initial rise, it turned and flew toward the far side of the field, about seventy-five feet away. When it was about twenty feet away from the guide, I fired, but the only effect my shot had was to double the bird's speed. Another twenty feet out I snapped off another shot, but with no effect at all. The guide's command to shoot when the bird was directly over him had rattled me so that my aim was off. I finally got myself in hand, took a deep breath, held it, swung onto the bird, passed it and fired in the middle of a smooth swing. The pheasant crumbled in mid-wingbeat and fell like a stone, just at the edge of the woods a full seventy-five feet away.

I was delighted, and blessed Bill for insisting on full choke guns. At that distance an open pattern would have been harmless. As I turned to be congratulated on the difficult shot I had made, I saw Bill chambering a shell. He had fired too! So the kill must have been his.

The dog trotted up to me with the bird held gently in her mouth. The guide took the cock from her and held it up for me to admire, but my triumph had gone. "It's Bill's," I said. "We both shot at the same time." Bill protested that he had been about to down the bird, but saw that I was on target and pulled up at the last minute. At first I didn't believe him, but I became more inclined to be convinced as I admired the bird—a beautiful, plump, ring-neck cock, bright russet-brown with black and white markings, black-flecked tan wings and tail and an iridescent emerald head, set off by a white ring around his neck. As I hefted him and felt that he would make a superb meal for four, I decided that Bill must be right—I had brought this beauty down.

The dog was already working again. She darted back and forth across the field in a short zigzagging pattern, looking and sniffing. Her coat was wet from the grass, and the dappled whiteness of it blended with the wet, yellow clumps. We walked behind her in a line across the field, the guide following close, Bill left of center, me off to the right. Despite the dog's tireless investigation, no birds were found in the length of the field. Then, at the very end, she came to point again, her nose aiming right at the center of a fifteen-foot-high clump of brush. Bill walked up and the guide went in to flush the quarry. A few minutes later, we heard the beating of wings and the tenacious bird burst out of cover, flying fast. Bill's gun was up and he dropped her just as she cleared the edge of the cover. The dog got back with the bird just as the guide reached us. The setter laid the pheasant at Bill's feet, then waited for the guide to brush the loose feathers from her mouth. This bird was a hen, lighter than mine. A meal for two.

We left our birds at the intersection of two trails where a jeep that circulated through the preserve would pick them up, then started toward the next field. The day was bright now and the leaves had begun to dry. A slight breeze was stirring the dogwoods to confetti. A puff of wind would turn up the bright pink leaves, and the silvery undersides would glisten and vibrate in the wind like shimmering disks of silver, or like bright light on rippling water. When the breeze stopped, they would instantaneously return to vivid pink, as if the wind were a switch that illuminated and extinguished the magic light of the dogwoods with an electric pulse.

There were great bushes of bittersweet berries, some plants spread twenty feet across, all thick and heavy with clusters of perfectly matched half-inch orange spheres. Their even, dull-surfaced, bright-colored tone made them look like two-dimensional graphics or stage sets against which the electrifying dogwoods staged a pyrotechnic ballet. The tall ash trees stood unmoved and uninvolved in the interplay of color on the forest floor, their trunks a grave intruding presence in the gay spectacle, their foliage a somber, subtly varying brown and yellow canopy over the bright frivolity beneath them.

The next field was a harvested cornfield. Ranks of brown, broken stalks marched along its two-hundred-yard length at half-yard intervals. The earth was bare, dull brown, with no cover but the desolate stalks. Once again I was sure no game could be there and once again was wrong as a dull brown hen pheasant rose up from the dull brown earth, the black markings on her feathers the same irregular black as the patterns of the shadows of the cornstalks. I fired three times, but she flapped off unscathed. The dog was in and working now and soon had a bird up for Bill. He connected on a long shot as the hen quartered across the field. By the time we had covered the area, I had harvested another fat hen and Bill brought down a sleek cock.

We decided to hunt through some thin woods on our way back to the lodge. The shooting here would be more difficult—birds could burst from cover and take cover again without crossing a clear patch of sky. The first bird flushed at the edge of a small valley. Bill shot and missed and the pheasant flew down into the bush below. The guide and Bill took the dog down to flush him out while I covered the ridge. I heard loud beating wings and turned around

to see a pheasant flying right at me, about twenty feet away. I slapped off a shot and the cock crumpled at my feet. I picked up my trophy and rushed down to tell Bill about the incredibly difficult shot I had made.

When I got there, I found him and the guide dumfounded. The dog would go on point, hold, break, move forward, point again and repeat the cycle. Four or five times a minute the confused animal would move her position ten or twenty feet forward, point, wait and hold again. We followed along mystified. The pheasant was literally *running* away from us. It was the same bird Bill had shot at and missed, so we knew that it *could* fly. It just seemed to know that the rules of the game called for shooting only flying birds, and so elected to retreat on foot. We followed along much more out of curiosity than from any desire to shoot the crafty hen, and she led us on a quarter-mile walk in twenty-foot spurts, until she finally *climbed* into a tall pine tree, hopping up from branch to branch, careful not to boost herself by flapping her wings and thus become a legitimate target.

The poor dog was more than a little perplexed. The basic working order of her world wasn't functioning, although she had done her part perfectly. She smelled the bird, pointed, ran forward to flush. But instead of the wingbeats and loud report and soft dead bird to retrieve and feathers to spit out, the bird walked away from her. And then climbed a tree. She looked dazed and then went into a fit of barking. This breach of pheasant hunting etiquette was extraordinary from so polite a dog, and we decided that the experience had taxed her nerves a bit and that it was time to go in. Our first five birds had been picked up by the jeep in its regular circuits of the trails, but my last, the difficult head shot, dangled proudly from my belt as I told and retold the story of the fast shot. Our legs were tired now and our shoulders aware of the blows laid on the hundred blows of the day before. It had been a relatively slow morning for a preserve hunt, but had provided just the right amount of action for opening our season. When we got back to the office-lounge, we indulged ourselves in one of the most delicious luxuries of hunting on a preserve: we exchanged our birds for some shot several weeks before and cleaned, hung, plucked and frozen. Our bag would go to some hunters two weeks hence. It was with some reluctance that I parted with the head-shot cock, but the thought of the time and work that would be necessary before he would become pheasant à la crême won out, and I swapped him for a neatly trussed package that would be our dinner three days later.

Although we had pampered ourselves with a preserve hunt this year, we usually hunt pheasant in the fields around our summer home. The same rituals are observed, but often not to the same degree. The dog we borrow may point and flush, but not retrieve. More likely he will only flush, and decide that any birds he finds on the ground are his.

We still take turns walking up on birds, but since the opportunities for shots are fewer, we're always sure to back up each other's shots.

Almost any field of a couple of acres or more is a good starting place for pheasant. If the field is a picked-over cornfield or has rye grass or other food, all the better. There need not be much to eat; just the seeds of wild grasses are enough.

We start at one end of the field and walk parallel paths through it, keeping the dog crisscrossing in front of us. We almost always find a bird or two in each field, and have learned to observe the pheasants' feeding and traveling times so that a bit of extra work in driving from field to field will yield a catch almost as full as that at the preserve.

The main disadvantage of a non-preserve hunt is that we have to clean and pluck our own bag, but even that has a positive side. Although no one actually enjoys plucking, it produces two very desirable products: a naked pheasant, ready for smoking or marinating, and a pile of feathers, ready to cover almost anything with elegance. We use this bonus for evening shoes, hatbands, throw rugs, picture frames, and vests, and even frame the feathers themselves, intact on the whole cured pheasant skin.

Whether we intend to marinate or smoke a pheasant, we start by eviscerating the carcass and hanging the bird in plumage for five days. It must be hung where no sun will reach it, and the temperature must not exceed 36 degrees during the hanging period.

After hanging, the pheasant is plucked, and either smoked over hickory for twenty-four hours or marinated for five days in wine, vinegar and herbs. If it has been marinated, we bake it in a cream

sauce to complete the melding of the tastes of wine and meat or serve it roasted, elegantly decorated in full plumage.

We reserve Smoked Pheasant for especially gala evenings. The pheasant is carved in the thinnest possible slices and arranged in meticulously regular rows, rich brown edges overlapping each preceding pure white slice, around a sprig of fresh crabapple, bright with tiny orange-red fruit, rich in emerald leaves. It is a supremely elegant hors d'oeuvre or, preceded by Pheasant Pâté and served with a red Burgundy, a superb after-theater supper. We serve Smoked Pheasant with Currant Sauce, which does not interfere with the subtle interplay of the flavors of the delicate flesh and rough hickory which are among the finest rewards of the pheasant harvest.

Because the harvest is always so abundant, pheasant is one of our staple foods each fall and winter. We use it for everything from simple dinners for just us, to our most formal entertaining. At least once a year we have a pheasant feast for our friends, especially those with the least venturesome palates. Pheasant is the perfect introduction to the appreciation of game since it is the least gamy of all wild things. The taste is almost that of a domestic fowl with only the slightest lacing of the special flavor of the wild. But under the wine and cream, masked, but not obliterated, is that slight strain, that infinitesimal hint of wildness. And that hint can be enough to pique the taste and curiosity of the uninitiated and lead to the opening of the realms of exquisite tastes of wild things, or to be sought and found under its condiment shield by the appreciating palates of lifelong game lovers.

Feasting on Pheasant

Hanging a Pheasant

After the pheasant hunt, eviscerate bird and sprinkle cavity generously with salt. Hang pheasant in plumage in shaded, airy spot, preferably under north eaves of house for 5 days. Temperature must never exceed 36 degrees during aging. If temperature rises, conclude aging in refrigerator, hanging bird from highest rack and removing lower racks.

Cut off head and wings and pull out tail feathers, leaving all intact. Reserve these in airtight plastic bag. Keep refrigerated.

Pluck bird, saving every single marked feather for decorative uses later.

Marinate bird in Basic Game Marinade for from 3 to 5 days.

Pheasant Liver Dressing

Pheasant liver, minced
2 tablespoons butter
1 small onion, finely chopped
1 stalk celery, finely chopped
2 medium mushrooms, chopped
½ cup 2-day-old bread
  chopped into small cubes
¼ teaspoon sage
⅛ teaspoon thyme
Salt
Freshly ground pepper
1 teaspoon chopped fresh parsley
½ teaspoon dried basil
4 tablespoons chicken stock
2 eggs

In butter, lightly sauté onion, celery and mushrooms. When transparent and golden, add minced liver and cook 1 minute, stirring carefully with a wooden spoon.

Mix together remaining ingredients.

Combine with sautéed mixture. Stuff and truss bird.

Roast Pheasant Decorated in Plumage

Wrap thin strips of bacon around pheasant, "mummy" fashion. Encase bird completely, placing large chunks of butter under bacon strips. This assures tender, juicy pheasant.

Place bird in covered roasting pan and roast for 2 hours in a moderate (350 degree) oven.

Remove bacon strips, baste with drippings and roast in uncovered pan for additional 25 minutes, basting every 5 minutes.

Serve pheasant on silver platter, elegantly garnished with head, wings and tail feathers, which have been reserved.

Serve with Sour Cream Sauce and Polenta.

Polenta

1 cup water-ground corn meal
4¾ cups cold water
1 teaspoon salt
1 juniper berry
Pinch of paprika
Pinch of red pepper
½ cup grated Parmesan cheese

Combine corn meal, ¾ cup water, salt and juniper and stir well. Bring 4 cups water to brisk boil; stir in corn-meal mixture a little at a time.

Cook, stirring constantly, over quick heat for 5 minutes.

Remove juniper berry.

Add paprika, pepper and cheese.

Place in double boiler over gently boiling water and continue cooking and stirring for 5 minutes.

Cover tightly, turn off heat and allow to steam over hot water for 10 minutes.

Sour Cream Sauce

4 tablespoons butter
¼ cup finely minced shallots
½ cup dry white wine
2 juniper berries
2 tablespoons potato flour
2 cups chicken stock
3 mushrooms, finely slivered
Pinch of nutmeg
Salt
Freshly ground black pepper
1 cup sour cream

Melt 2 tablespoons butter in skillet, add shallots and sauté gently. Add wine and juniper berries and cook slowly until mixture reduces. Remove juniper berries.

In top of enamel double boiler, combine 2 tablespoons butter and potato flour. When smoothly blended add chicken stock and stir over low heat until mixture thickens. Add mushrooms. Decrease amount of boiling water in bottom of double boiler. Simmer sauce gently for 1 hour, stirring frequently.

Strain, and season with nutmeg, salt and pepper.

Stir in shallot mixture and simmer gently for about 7 minutes. Place sour cream in a separate bowl and spoon in a small quantity of the hot sauce. Add ¼ teaspoon salt and blend. This will prevent curdling when cream is combined with boiling sauce.

Add cream to sauce, blend, and simmer gently for 2 minutes.

Remove to heated sauce boat and serve with Roast Pheasant and Polenta.

Pheasant in Cream

1 pheasant, hung and marinated	1 tablespoon finely chopped shallots
4 tablespoons butter	½ teaspoon thyme
4 tablespoons olive oil	1 bay leaf
½ cup finely chopped carrots	½ cup white wine
½ cup finely chopped celery	4 tablespoons cognac
½ cup finely chopped onions	2 cups heavy cream

Brown pheasant all over in foaming butter and olive oil. Add carrots, celery, onions, shallots, thyme, and bay leaf. Simmer for 2 minutes. Add wine. Cover and bake in moderate oven (350 degrees) for 1 hour. Pour off fat; flame pheasant with heated cognac. Add cream and return to oven for ½ hour. Remove bird to heated serving dish. Strain sauce. Add salt and pepper. Reduce over medium heat until sauce is quite thick. Pour over pheasant.

Pheasant Pâté

1 pheasant, marinated
1 pound lean fresh pork
½ pound fat fresh pork
1 egg, beaten
1 bay leaf
Salt
3 tablespoons reserved marinade
10 thin slices fat salt pork
Pâté dough
1 cup very firm jellied white stock

2 tablespoons Madeira
1 teaspoon gelatin dissolved in 2 tablespoons cold water

Remove breasts of marinated pheasant and cut into 12 very thin slices. Reserve.

Trim bones of remaining meat and remove all sinews.

Combine trimmings with lean and fat pork.

Put through finest grading of food chopper twice.

Place the finely chopped meat in a bowl.

Mix with egg, crumbled bay leaf and salt.

Add reserved marinade and mix thoroughly.

In terrine lined with baked Pâté Dough (next recipe) arrange thin salt pork slices on bottom and sides.

Place ⅓ of the chopped-meat mixture evenly on bottom and lay 6 slices of pheasant breast on top.

Repeat, ending with chopped-meat mixture.

Cover with remaining slices of salt pork.

Cover with reserved rolled-out Pâté Dough. Dampen bottom rim and press ends firmly together.

Insert a waxed-paper tube into small hole in top crust to allow steam to escape.

Set terrine in pan of hot water and bake in a 425-degree oven for one hour.

Reduce heat to 375 degrees and bake one hour longer.

While pâté is cooling, heat white stock.

Remove from heat; add Madeira and dissolved gelatin.

Allow to cool slightly.

Pour through waxed-paper vent into pheasant pâté.

Cool pâté thoroughly, letting it set. Serve in slices.

38

Pâté Dough

4 cups flour
¾ cup butter
1¼ cups lard
1 egg
½ cup iced water
1 teaspoon salt

Mix ingredients together, handling dough very gently.

Wrap in waxed paper and refrigerate overnight.

Roll ¾ of the dough into large oval shape to a thickness of ⅛ inch. Roll out at least an inch larger than mold to allow for shrinkage.

The pheasant hunt is a ceremony; every motion, every method has had generations of faithful observance and practice.

Pheasant is the perfect introduction to the appreciation of game since it is the least gamey of all wild things.

Double the dough on moistened rim and press firmly all around. Bake for 10 minutes in a 450-degree oven.

Roll out remaining dough to ¼-inch thickness, 1 inch larger around than terrine top. Reserve.

Smoked Pheasant

1 pheasant (hung for 5 days)
¾ cup brown sugar
¾ cup coarse salt
6 cloves
2 gallons cold water

Pluck and singe the pheasant.

Prepare brine of brown sugar, coarse salt and cloves and water in earthen or stone crock.

Keep pheasant in brine for 48 hours.

Remove pheasant and allow to "drip-dry" for several hours.

Arrange briquettes of charcoal in pit of smokehouse or in smoking barrel. Allow to turn red.

Add more charcoal when it ignites.

Add 2 green or dampened hickory logs. When they begin to smolder, insert sturdy wire through center of pheasant (from wing to wing). Fashion hook at end of wire and hang bird from elevated crossbar.

Add a log at a time during smoking. Do not allow logs to flame. This can be controlled by adding fresh charcoal from time to time as required.

Smoke for 24 hours.

Keep in cool, dry place. Do not refrigerate.

Currant Sauce

¼ cup currants
1 tablespoon brown sugar
1 tablespoon vinegar
1 cup brown sauce

Pour boiling water over currants until they become plump. Drain and reserve.

Place sugar and vinegar in pan and brown.

Blend in brown sauce; boil for several minutes, stirring constantly.

Remove from heat and add plumped currants.

Chapter 4.
The Boar and Bear Adventure

A boar hunt is for men. A bear hunt is for supermen. And I was about to do both. As an accolade for my mastering the skills and rituals of hunting during the course of several seasons after deer, waterfowl and upland game, Bill decided to take me to the Smoky Mountains in North Carolina for Russian boar and black bear. It was an intimidating adventure from the start.

On all of our previous hunts we had used guns from the collection Bill had assembled over years of hunting. It had always seemed that he had two of every firearm there was. But the formidable game we were about to pursue required more formidable armament than anything in his arsenal. The new guns were fantastic: Remington semi-automatic .30-06 rifles. I had long since learned to have a great respect for all firearms, but these commanded a very special sort of awe. They looked no larger, no more complex, than other guns I had shot. Their impressiveness came from their straightforward functionality. Six and a half pounds of walnut and steel that would fire 180-grain partially metal jacketed lead projectiles as quickly as the plain steel triggers were squeezed. These were lethal guns, for potentially lethal game.

The week before the hunt we went to a range to get accustomed to our new rifles. The factory had calibrated the sights for accuracy at fifty yards, and, although I knew it was close, it was chilling to see just how close it was. And fifty yards was the longest shot we were likely to get.

The ammunition matched the purposefulness of the guns: two-and-quarter-inch tubes of brass, tipped with a three-quarter-inch lead bullet. I loaded four into the clip, put one into the chamber, closed the action, put in the clip and was set.

Gun up, safety off. The noise was incredible. The shot stunned my ears so, I could hear only its own instant echo from the earth bank behind the target and the steady ringing of the reverberations within my ears. The first shot wasn't bad. Two inches off the two-inch bull's eye we'd set as our standard. I shot again—badly now, nine inches high. Once more, and once more well over, flinching in anticipation of the blast. I started to take myself in hand, realizing that I had flinched, taking a minute to get over it, when on my left, five explosions roared out so quickly that the space between the shock of the sounds was filled with the shock of their echoes. Bill had done better than I. His five fast shots were all

within two inches of the bull. I steadied myself and tried again, reminding myself of shooting basics. Steady . . . breathe in . . . hold breath . . . squeeze. This time it was better. We shot for about a half hour, until we could group five shots within two inches of the bull in the five seconds it would take a boar or bear to cover the distance between us and the targets. The longest shot we could expect would be that short: fifty yards. The rhododendron and laurel would screen anything beyond that range. If the cover was thick we might have only twenty yards—two or three seconds—to place our shots before the animal was on top of us.

We flew south on a Sunday morning—and then we drove. The lodge was in wilderness, two fast-driving, rainy hours from the nearest airport, through mountains which were unlike any others I had ever seen. Instead of forming lines of ridges they formed a random pattern of individual peaks. Each mountain was a cone with creaselike radial ridge lines running from the base to a pointed crest. They were covered with silver birch trees and thickets of shiny wet rhododendron and laurel. The glistening green banks of leaves rose straight up on either side of the road so that all that could be seen was the slick, black asphalt and the foliage and the grey mist above, as if the serpentine road was a path defined by the space between two gigantic, wet, green-scaled snakes, their hiss the hiss of the tires on wet pavements. Occasionally the solid green curtains would be ripped open by massive, jagged rocks, steeper than even the steepness of the green-covered mountains. Sometimes a river would parallel the road. But the greatest part of the drive was spent hurtling along between two unbroken banks of green.

Then the road changed. Instead of slithering around the bases of the mountains we were going right up one. There were no straight stretches at all as the road doubled back on itself repeatedly, to attack the slope at a gentler angle. We were following the Blue Boar Lodge's signs now—wooden placards at every intersection (and along the longer unbroken stretches to keep up morale)—and suddenly one of them pointed straight down over the edge of the mountain. We stopped and saw a small dirt drive, now liquid mud and slush, winding down into the hollow between two radial ridge spines. That last half-mile took fifteen minutes. Some of the turns were too sharp to navigate in one motion. We had to turn, back up, turn again, all on wet loose gravel and mud bordered by sheer drops of hundreds of feet. The foliage was so thick that we didn't see the lodge until we turned a corner and were in its yard. And as soon as we turned that corner we were at home.

The family that ran the lodge seemed to think that we were long-lost kin. There was a warm welcome in our rooms, heated up in anticipation of our arrival, in the waiting coffee and the massive fireplace in the main room, and beaming from our hosts.

We were on a special hunt, since no women but the owner's wife and daughter are allowed at the lodge during the main hunting season. But aside from my female presence, everything was exactly as usual. After we got settled into our room it was time for dinner. The food in most hunting camps is always good and hearty, but this was far beyond most. The owner had run a restaurant until two years before, and sold it to buy the lodge simply because he loved the life. That appreciation of the way he lived was in everything he did. He knew the flowers that bloomed in a steady sequence each spring. He knew the beauties and exhilarations of the chase. He gloried in sharing the best times, the vacation times, with all of his guests and in effect vacationing every week of the year, even if it was a vacation on which he worked a solid twelve-hour day six days a week. The joy that he found in this life gave him and his family and his home, for the lodge was really that, a very beautiful aura of contentment into which every guest was drawn.

After dinner we gathered in the main room of the lodge for a briefing on the next day's hunt. We would leave the lodge at six in the morning and drive to the area to be hunted. Once there we would use an area stand method—each hunter would be assigned an area rather than a specific spot. Each area would be cut off from those next to it by some solid earth—a hill or a curve in a logging road—since the heavy bullets we would be using could carry for half a mile through the brush. The younger of our two guides would drive toward the stand with a pack of hounds while the older one checked on hunters along the line.

When the hounds pick up a trail they begin to bark, and we were to adjust our positions within our stand area according to the direction of their sound. We were told to listen for the difference between the melodious and moving trail bark, and the short and sharp still bay bark, and that if we heard the dogs bring the boar to bay near our stands that we were to move up for the kill.

We were to be ready for game even if we heard a shot, as the dogs often run several boar at once, and occasionally run bear with the boar. Deer were not to be shot, however, as the hounds would then think that they were desirable quarry, and be ruined for boar and bear.

Next we were told about the game. Black bear is more dangerous than boar. If a bear is startled he will probably tree. If one did, we would have to shoot very carefully, for a treed bear must be killed instantly with one shot between the eyes. When a bear is wounded he drops out of his tree onto the dogs, making it difficult or impossible to get in another shot. He will certainly kill some dogs and very possibly attack and kill the hunter. Should a bear come to bay on the ground he presents a much more difficult shot, as the hounds will be all around him and he will be moving much more quickly as he fights. In that case the guide (who will almost certainly get there first) will say where and when to shoot.

With boar, shot placement need not be quite so precise, but there is one complication. The Russian boar's coat is a combination of bristle and fur that stands straight up when he is excited. This means that he looks about four inches bigger all around than he actually is, and that what would seem to be a fatal spine shot will pass harmlessly through the standing pelt. The best shot from the side is at the apparent center of the shoulder, and since the boar's shoulders are protected by an inch-thick armorplate of gristle, only large-caliber guns can be used. A head-on shot is more difficult. The boar must be hit between the bases of his ears, and he will probably be moving fast. The four-inch tusks on the head over the fireplace looked very ominous as our host explained that because of his wedge shape a boar can penetrate the laurel and tangleweed faster than a deer, and that we would have perhaps a second or two to get off a shot.

We were given the signal for help, one shot, count to ten, two shots, repeated every half hour; told that if lost we were to walk downhill until we found any trickle of water, then follow that water until we got to a road and wait there to be picked up; and finally warned to be very careful in picking our targets, as boar, bear and some dogs are black.

At six, we were out to meet the guides and their dogs. The guides almost bolted when they saw me. They are very conservative men, not given to changing their habits. They had never hunted with a woman and saw no reason to start. The entire idea was anathema to them. Hunting was a man's business. Hard. Basic. And there I was in a leather miniskirt and red tam-o'-shanter. They just wouldn't hear of it. For a while we thought the adventure was to be called off, but Bill spun some powerful yarns about my previous hunting experience and our host persuaded them to give it a try. The men were amazing. We were about to put our lives quite literally into their care, and they inspired such complete and immediate confidence that we had no reservations about doing it. There was nothing superfluous about them—no fat, no muscle beyond what was needed to run ten miles through thickets in an hour and a half, just a utilitarian hard leanness.

The dogs mirrored the economical, functional look of their masters. There were chase dogs—plot hounds, redbones, Norwegian elk hounds, Walkers and combinations of some or all of the breeds. As puppies they were thrown into pens with captive boars to be roughed up and develop a boar killing instinct. They keep that instinct sharp by hunting every day of the year, despite the fact that the season is only open for four months. They will chase a boar or bear all day if necessary, and once it is brought to bay they will hold it there for days unless they're called off or the boar is killed.

The catch dogs were pit bulls, huskier and covered with scars. These dogs follow the chase dogs on pursuit, then when the boar or bear is brought to bay, they come up, pick an opening on the game, and attack. While the hounds hold the game at bay, encircling it, barking and rushing in and nipping, the pit bulls bite just once, then hold on until the quarry is dead or they are. One swipe of a boar's tusk, our host told us, will open a foot-and-a-half-long gash down a dog's belly, but the dog will hang on even as its intestines fall out. More incredible, the eviscerated dog will probably be clamped just as determinedly on another boar a week later. Most of the injuries happen when a boar comes to bay with its back protected in a stream, a dense laurel bush or against a tree.

Some hounds are caught when they back into a tree after nipping in to worry a pig, and almost any time a bear is bayed rather than treed, dogs are hurt. All the guides carry sterilized needles and thread, and when a dog is gashed, they simply push in whatever innards have come out and sew the animal back together.

Although they seem to have no affection at all for their dogs (most of the hounds have never been inside a house, and all of them are casually fed and go into fits of delight if spoken to or petted), the guides will drive for hours to get to a vet if one of their animals is too seriously injured to be patched up in the field. The guides do give the dogs respect—the special respect of courageous, competent men for courageous, competent partners in a dangerous trade.

We were to watch that trade from a distance on the first day of the hunt. Two or three hunters are allowed to work with the driving guide each day, following the dogs, but since I was lucky to be allowed even in the woods, we contented ourselves with taking a stand. We drove along a dirt logging road for about half an hour, then walked. The woods looked like a solid thicket, but the guide seemed to know an easy path through all of it. The site of the stands was a line of hills, and we were stationed in the depressions between the ridges. Bill and I took a stand together, although it halved our chances of getting a boar, and the guide seemed relieved that the first woman he'd ever taken into the field would be with someone who seemed to know what he was doing.

For the first half hour we patrolled our stand. We were halfway up the crease between two ridge lines of a medium-small hill. The depression was about two hundred feet across, widening to three hundred down at the base. Below us was a small clearing, and below that and up the opposite hill, laurel and greenbriar thicket. Behind us dense green rhododendron piled up and covered the top of our hill. We tried to figure likely paths a boar would take across the valley even though we knew his low-nosed, wedge shape could penetrate any of the thicket as easily as we could run across an open field. The clearing in front of us was only about twenty yards wide, and we both felt (though neither voiced) some worry about being able to get off a shot in the time it would take a two-hundred-pound boar with razor tusks to cross it. Bill could not smoke, as the hogs have an excellent sense of smell, but we indulged all of our other nervous tics completely. I paced a bit and studied rocks. We talked quietly, of silly yet serious things: "Couple pigged to death" seemed a possible joint obituary. We checked and re-checked our guns. Safety on. Clip in. Action closed and ready to shoot. And all the time one of us watched the woods, peering, scanning, checking, until the other had finished with nervous twitching for a bit and could take over.

The dogs sounded miles away (as we later found they were). Rich musical howls seemed to float over the air. We strained our eyes and ears, watching the ridge a quarter mile away, seeing nothing but its vague outline through the thicket, perceiving the action taking place two miles away by its sounds alone.

We could tell the voices of the different dogs as they bayed, hear the shifts in direction. Some seemed to be off to the sides of the pack—perhaps several boar were coming. The excitement built with the growing volume of the musical howling. The hunt was being decided out there, and we, the hunters, could only stand and fidget. The music rose and fell as the dogs crossed ridges and went into valleys, and was becoming steadily louder. For five minutes the chase went on, then the barking changed. The sweet, melodious howls became short, vicious barks and snarls. The chase had stopped. The sound was close, but muffled. We checked our safeties and ran down into the valley. It was still beyond us. We scrambled up the ridge we had been facing, greenbriar holding us, pulling, blocking. As we cleared the top we could hear the dogs clearly—and in close. They were somewhere in the valley below us, holding the boar at bay. The younger guide burst over the top of the far ridge and charged down into the valley to our left, and we slid and ran through the brush in that direction. The snarling and yapping were closer—we could see the guide, then hear him as he called us in.

The boar had come to bay in a small clearing next to a stream. He was like a hill of bristling slate, lowered head and narrow haunches broadening out into a massive bulge of muscle in the lump over his shoulders. That hill was propped on fast and agile legs, and defended by two deadly tusks. Each move the dogs made was countered by a rush, a retreat or a cutlass slash of the boar's head. He gave no ground, showed no opening to the dogs, but

waited for them to come to him or for the opportunity to break for a better place to make his stand. The fight was feints and counterfeints. Dogs slipped in, then jumped back as a tusk flashed at them. No catch dog had been able to get in. The boar darted forward, turned, turned again—swinging his head like a spiked club, keeping the dogs back with his four-inch razors. Then, at the end of one turn he bolted forward and into the stream. He came to bay again in the water, his rump safe against one mossy bank, his slate black almost invisible under the deep black shadows. Two dogs leaped in after him, one downstream, one up. The others stood on the opposite bank and snarled. "He'll stand now," yelled the guide. "Move in for your shot." I was horrified to feel Bill pushing me forward for the kill. The dogs had obscured the boar and his darting and slashing made the shot doubly hard.

I ran upstream to get a clear side target, with as few dogs as possible in the way. One hound was just downstream and behind, another off a bit to one side when I clicked the safety off. I aimed at where the boar's spine should be, lowered four inches to allow for the standing hair, and squeezed. The blast ricocheted around the valley, but for a second nothing happened. I aimed for a second shot when the boar fell.

The dogs all leaped at once, swarming over the carcass until it was nothing but a mass of writhing, splashing hounds. I clicked on my safety and ran up. Bill and the guide were already there. The guide shooed off the dogs, and he and Bill began dragging the boar up the near bank.

I was thrilled and startled by my kill. He was much larger than he had appeared when crouched at bay—almost six feet from snout to outstretched hind legs. Bill and the guide strained to get him out of the stream. Finally when he was halfway up the bank, they stopped and stepped back to admire the carcass. I was delighted when the guide allowed that, female or not, I had done some good shooting.

They slit the pig from the breastbone to the neck to let him drain, and the green moss bank was covered with glossy red. The brook flowed transparent crimson with the fast flowing blood.

The other guide came up then, and hunters began to drift in. The hog was a heavy animal, but we decided to pole him out. The younger guide castrated the carcass and continued the bleeding slit down to the tail. The steaming pink and white entrails were given to the dogs, we slung the pig on a two-inch sapling, and the lodge owner, Bill and I headed back. It was still early, so the other hunters would try another stand before joining us. Back at the lodge the boar was hung up for snapshots, then left to drain. We decided to wait to skin it until the other hunters got back so those who were so inclined could have their own pictures taken with it, in case they didn't connect.

Two hours later another boar was hanging next to ours, and every camera in camp was busy recording every hunter and combination of hunters with the trophies. The crowd seemed to evaporate into mist when it was time for the skinning.

Each hog was cut down, and the successful hunters and the two guides started the long, hard peel. Since Bill and I had hunted as a team and I had taken on the duty of the shot, I thought it only fair that he share the work and deferred the skinning to him.

Each man started with a couple of sharp hunting knives and whetstones—they would be doing a lot more sharpening than actual skinning. They hacked off the rear hooves and made a split down the back leg to the gutting slit in the abdomen. Then a little knife sharpening. Next the skin was peeled off the rear legs (more pulling than cutting here) and the peeling started up the carcass.

And a little more knife sharpening. The boar has one of the toughest hides of all animals, and the toughest part was coming. The cutting and pulling reached the rib area, where the gristle armor starts. Here each inch or two of skinning called for the whetstone. This gristle is protection for the boar's mating season fights, in which contesting males stand facing in opposite directions, shoulder to shoulder, and swing their heads like wrecking balls into each other's rib cages, tusk first. Their lower tusks are honed by the grinding action of the uppers, whose only function is to sharpen the lowers every time the boar opens and closes his mouth. When ours was clean to the head, we stopped: this beauty was for the taxidermist. We just cut the head and cape off and sent it to a nearby town for mounting.

Next, we put the boar into a giant barrel of brine to soak for a day to get out the excess blood. The brine was changed every few hours, and with each change, the discarded brine was a lighter shade of pink.

50   The next day the guides complimented my marksmanship and woods savvy by inviting us to run with them. We had heard that the previous day's selected hunters had staggered to the site of my kill a full half hour after we had started back, and had spent the rest of the hunt sprawled in two of the cars, but we decided to accept.

The hunt started, as before, with a drive by car deep into the woods, but when the main convoy stopped we went on for another mile. There were two guides handling dogs that day, and a larger pack than the day before, to better the chances of a multiple start. The beginning of the boar drive was like a nature walk. There was none of the jitteriness of the day before. The hounds fanned out in a line and trotted forward slowly, chase dogs loitering behind. The guides were split on either side of the center of the line, Bill and I with the one on the left, another veteran, the brother of the first, on the right. We walked briskly through the woods, careful to go around the greenbriar, not bothering to scan the underbrush for game. The dogs would start the hunt if it was to start, and we had nothing to do but walk behind and listen to the guide. He was a taciturn man, but with a lot to say. My change from the previous day's leather miniskirt to hunting pants was noted with "Dressed sensible today." "Greenbriar" and a sparse gesture showed us the easy way through the brush, though even that could not help us move through the woods with his effortless aplomb. The only time enough sentences came close enough together to become paragraphs was when the conversation turned to the dogs or the game—and then the economical trickle of words became a torrent. Every strength and every foible of every dog in the pack was enumerated. The probable reaction of a boar to any challenge was detailed—as were the various less probable, but possible, responses. We learned the boar's eating habits, ranging patterns, sleeping times. We learned that the food where we were was plentiful this year, so there was a good chance of doubles. As we drove toward the stands of hunters watched over by the father and teacher of our guide, we were hearing the distilled essence of a lifetime of accumulated lore built on generations of hunting experience.

We moved through changing light and changing foliage as we circled the bases of the small hills. (No need to go over their tops —the dogs would find game if it was there.) The patterns were of shadows, not of light—pure black and deepest green as we passed between two hills heaped with rhododendron, dappled grey and forest-floor brown flickering through the laurel bushes in the hollows, long early-morning shadows of silver birch broken only by slashes of light. No need for silence, no reason not to smoke. We were driving boar, not waiting for them.

A howl off to our right, then a chorus, drew our dogs and our guide almost out of our sight before we could react to their leaving. We ran to follow, desperate, but slower. The guide would not wait if we could not keep up—to hold back would jeopardize the hunt for everyone else. There was no skirting the hills now. We followed the barks and crashing of bushes up and over hills, down through valleys, through the thickets. The pack turned, and we angled off to intercept them. Two steep hillocks later, we were momentarily with our guide again, but no boar was in sight. The dogs were just ahead, but flanking, rather than following, the boar, to pick up any others with him who might otherwise escape by turning off. We scrambled around a hill just in time to hear the dogs turn again and see the guide disappear around another ridge line. His shout came back around the corner. "Hurry, they've jumped a bear.'' It seemed impossible that he could run so and still have breath to shout, for our fumbling rush had left me gasping.

We angled across again, legs never stopping their frenzied, sometimes futile, scrambling up hills. Rushing, stopped short by briar, pushing through, backing off and running, constantly running.

We were heading away from the stand hunters. This bear was ours or no one's. The barking was about two ridges ahead, the crashing brush an indeterminate distance, but still it was a sound we could follow.

All of the excitement of the day before came back many times over in an exhilarating combination of the thrill of pursuit and fear of the bear we were pursuing. Our legs churned like berserk machines as we slipped and slid and pulled ourselves up hills, hand over hand on the birch trunks. We clawed the steep hills' crust to try to reach the tops a second sooner. We were gasping hard, trying to force enough air into our lungs to drive our failing legs.

The sound changed, but not to the vicious bay bark. They were coming toward us! The shock of fear redoubled, and redoubled my straining. They were two ridges away, then just a valley and a ridge. We could hear the crashing brush over the crashing we made.

We forced ourselves up the next ridge and were about to start down the other side when we saw the bear, forty feet off, and right in our paths. He stopped when he saw us, and was instantly surrounded by the dogs. No shot would be safe now, with dogs all around the bear keeping him at bay. The dogs would momentarily back off to expose an amorphous black mass with a vivid pink spot that was his roaring, biting, mouth. A gigantic swipe of a paw would split the air. White claws and white fangs flashed.

While the dogs and foliage still prevented a shot, we slipped off to the side and joined up with the guide just as the bear broke cover and ran up past the spot we had held, with the pack not five feet behind. Again we ran, legs churning, lungs searing, chest burning, driving hard just to keep up. Hillsides were half run, half slid. We pumped our legs a bit longer, a bit farther. Then, on the ridge beyond, the bear bayed again—a vague black shape in the rhododendron's black shadows. But there was never a chance for a shot—the bear was covered by dogs. He broke out, and again the dogs and guide were after him. We strained behind, now seeing the bear through a bush, now seeing a patch of dog.

Two bays and no possible shot. Our legs thrashed on as the dogs moved farther ahead. Pain shot through my chest, pain from the running and pain from the fear. The dogs were two ridges ahead. Greenbriar caught and stopped me. Disentangle. Push. Run. Now Bill was half a hill ahead of me, the dogs a hill ahead of him. We ran and gasped and climbed and gripped and pulled and pushed ourselves one hill further. The forest seemed to clear beyond a ridge, and Bill had stopped at the top. I used my last energy to get up to him, then sank to the ground. The guide was just below the crest, hunched down watching. The dogs stood twenty feet below him, milling and barking. A hundred feet beyond them swam the bear straight out across the lake that broke the seemingly endless series of hills, a catch dog clamped onto his back as he swam. A shot now and the bear would sink. The far side was Tennessee, where the bear season had already closed. When the big black was two hundred feet out, the guide called back the pit bull, and the animal, which would have stayed clamped onto the bear until death, let go and came immediately to his master's voice.

I lay still, racked with the searing of my lungs, needing more air than even this open-sky country seemed to have. Bill sat down and gasped. The guide quietly went about examining his dogs and patching up minor cuts.

After a few minutes, we started a slow walk back. We had run for two unbroken hours. When we got to the cars, we found the others ready to leave. Their hunt had been a long one and the dogs were too tired to start again.

Back at the lodge we started preparations for barbecuing our boar. First we dug a fire pit and drove in two forked tree-trunk uprights on either side of it. Then we piled heavy hickory logs over a base of fast-burning pine and started the fire. By the time we had the boar out of brine and bound to a two-inch-thick greenwood spit, the pine had burned off, leaving the long-burning hickory flaming and turning to coals.

We slung the spit between the uprights and went to dinner. Before bed, we went back to turn the spit. The boar had roasted upside down for four hours. Now we built up a blaze that would last till dawn and turned the hog upright, to sear and roast the inside of the chest cavity and lower flanks. While we stoked up the fire the darkness intensified the effect of the firelight on the brown-seared flesh of the roasting boar. We sat to enjoy the fire and listen to its crackling in counterpoint to the quiet sounds of a brook nearby. The stillness of the tall birch woods around us was reinforced by the myriad stars that were a heavy glistening blanket in the clear black sky.

We sat absorbed in the small orange circle of firelight, surrounded by the large dark circle of the blackness of the woods, domed with the black sphere of sky alive with the incandescence of stars. The small sounds and great silences mesmerized us, and we might well have stayed until the light broke again, but another light, till now unperceived, went out. The lodge was turning in. As we walked back, we hurried a bit, anxious now for sleep. For we had a plan for the next day.

We were gone before the other hunters had finished breakfast. They would be hunting a new area that day. We were going back for the bear.

The guide had told us that the mast (the acorns and other edibles on the forest floor which are the staple food of both boar and bear) was very poor across the lake this year and that during the night, the bear would probably work his way back to the area in which we had found him.

We were in the field at six-thirty, this time alone. We were making our own hunt, with no dogs to find the game. We started working down from the logging road, toward the lake. It was about two miles away, but a day's stalking would never take us that far—especially since we planned to try to cover an area a quarter-mile wide.

We were silent. The only conversation was a few whispered words about the path to our first objective, a stand of oak about a quarter-mile into the woods.

We moved slowly into the brush, about a hundred feet apart. Each step took a half minute—a half minute of straining concentration, of peering into a deep shadow beneath a rhododendron, of looking back to see the sides of bushes that had been obscured the step

*It was a
heavy animal
but we decided
to pole
him out.*

Before bed, we went back to turn the spit. The boar had roasted upside down for four hours.

before, of scanning the hillside. Each new step was two seconds of straining concentration as we looked for noiseless bits of forest floor to plant our boots. Then we searched again, eyes dissecting the flanks of the hills around us. Each hollow was a potential lair. Every shadow could conceal a shadow-black bear.

Another step revealed a foot more on the far side of a dozen thickets—a foot of ground that might have just a claw of a bear on it, but we had to see that claw if we were to be successful.

We strained our eyes down the valley between the hills and up the hillsides. A laurel thicket a hundred feet away was a maze of branches and dappled shadows that needed several minutes of examination. And still each step had to be measured, each visible foot and inch examined each time a new step was taken.

We came to the first hill in our path and split up. We climbed up opposite sides, and walked along the length, about halfway from the top. The footing was precarious—sometimes a birch trunk would provide a brace for my foot, sometimes I would take fifteen seconds to find a quiet and secure place for my next step. The scanning was different now, and longer. I could see the crests of the hills beyond the one just across the valley. Every fold and bump of them needed examination. Each rock had to be studied to be sure it was a rock. Each bush must be peered into to be sure it hid no bear. The shadows and laurels and rhododendrons must be checked and checked and rechecked. And checked again at every step as every step revealed a new perspective.

I shuddered with a mixture of excitement, concentration and fear. Bill was on the other side of the hill. If the bear was in the valley below, he was mine—I had to find him. And I was sure he was there. I saw dozens of bears—bears that were rocks, bears that were shadows, bears that were no more than the rustle of a bush behind me that sent cold terror and a jolt of adrenalin all through my body.

Bill and I met at the end of the hill and began our next stalk toward the grove. Just ahead was a laurel thicket, and behind it a fairly open area of small hills sprinkled with greenbriar and thick with silver birch. We could see that the hills were clear, but a stream that coiled between them was surrounded by rhododendron and probably filled with trout—a perfect place for bear. We split up and crept around the laurel patch, peering in as best we could, but with no luck. We met on the far side, and Bill started down the stream bank while I climbed to the crest of the hills to one side. We could move a little faster here since the only place to watch was the rhododendron-covered bank. I scanned the hills around us and the valley ahead as we moved, but the end of every sweep was always the long line of heavy emerald bushes through which Bill was moving. Occasionally, I would see him through a break in the bushes, a bright yellow flash passing through the deep green. Then he would be absorbed again.

The stream ran past the oak grove we wanted to check, about a hundred feet to one side. Between the stream and the oaks the hills leveled off, and ground was covered with thicket. Bill stopped at the edge of the level spot and I went downstream to the far end of the small plain.

We moved very slowly now, picking our way around the thorns, peering into every bush, checking back to see the spots we could not see until we had passed them. In five minutes we reached the grove. Bill signaled me to skirt around my side of it and meet him at the game trail at the far end.

I turned deeper into the underbrush while Bill went around the other way. If the bear was there, he would probably be lying low on the edge of the grove. Every bush got complete attention, yet I was always marginally aware of every other bush as well. I could see for only ten yards—and I remembered how fast the bear I was now looking for had moved the day before. I picked my way around bushes expecting to find that mass of black flying at me behind slashing white fangs and claws from every one. I stopped to listen for rustling leaves or snapping twigs, in the wild, unreasonable hope that an animal that lived for years in these woods would move more clumsily than I did.

After an agonizingly cautious half hour Bill and I met at the game trail. Before moving on we checked over the grove, but there was no sign of a bear there that day.

We set off down the game trail, moving at almost a normal walking speed. Bill was scanning the left, I the right. The trail moved through tall foliage, but the plants were bare near the ground, so we could stoop under them and see a good distance at ground level. A quarter mile farther on—a half hour's fast stalking—

the trail curved around a brush-covered hill. We decided the hill
merited a look, and split up to go through it.

I stayed near the trail, circling the base of the hill while Bill cut
over the top. The going was slower now. Once more each bush
was a potential ambush spot, each shadow a possible bear. I
watched the trail by stooping and looking under the growth. Toward the hill, each plant required its own careful checking, since
their bottom leaves were not eaten or broken off. Bill and I re-
joined on the far side of the hill behind a dense thicket.

While up on the hill, Bill had noticed another stand of oak and
a small clearing just beyond the greenbriar and laurel. We walked
toward it in careful parallel paths through the thorns and branches.
Ten feet from the end of the brush, we saw the clearing, and found
a path that angled toward it.

We followed the path through a rhododendron maze to a spot just
off the center of the grove. We relaxed as we stepped into the
clearing, since we didn't expect to find the bear in the open. We
had taken a step toward some fresh scratch marks on one of the
trees when we heard and saw and sensed him all at once.

A blurred black mass was hurtling away from us across the grove.
At forty yards he paused and in that tiny pause we came out of
our immobilized shock. Our shots were fired before we knew our
guns were up. The bear dropped on the spot of his fatal indecision.
Then we ran. The bear was a beauty—he had just grown a soft,
long winter coat and was plump for hibernation. The thrill of
the catch mixed with awe of the powerful animal as we examined
our kill. Sharp three-inch claws formed rows of lethal rakes on
each powerful paw. Two-inch canine fangs studded the corners of
jaws powerful enough to snap a thighbone. He was a large bear
for this area, about six feet long and just a bit under three hundred pounds.

We were elated, and, after the elation, depleted. Our hunt lasted
six long, energy-burning hours. We had another hour's work before us, dragging the field-dressed bear to the nearest road. I
waited while Bill hiked for our car.

When we got back to the lodge, the other hunters were already
there. The photography session around their day's bag stopped
as soon as they saw us coming. We had plenty of help hanging
the carcass for skinning, and plenty of dumbfounded stares from

the guides who couldn't believe that a still hunt for bear had been successful with a woman as one of the hunters.

Bill and two guides skinned our trophy very carefully—the pelt would make a perfect rug. The steaks and loins were given the same brine soaking treatment we had given the boar, but were not barbecued. The barbecued pork was sent to a local smokehouse for two straight days of hickory smoking.

We left for home elated by the hard hunt we had successfully completed, exhilarated by the challenges against which we had pitted ourselves, and exhausted by the effort of it all. It seemed that we slept for days after getting home, but our trip had been harder on our guides than on us. They had no problem meeting the demands the hunt made on their strength or skill or courage. They were all overabundantly equipped with those qualities. The strain was on their traditions and their trust in their own sense and senses. When we left, a day after our bear hunt, there was still a more than slightly dumbfounded look on their faces over

the fact that a woman had survived a boar and bear hunt, that she hadn't shot another hunter, and, most incredible of all, that she had shot a Russian boar and a black bear. I half expect that when we return to the Blue Boar next year, we will find them all still grouped at the end of the driveway, staring with total disbelief in the direction of our departing car.

If a boar hunt is for men and a bear hunt for supermen, a boar and bear feast is for heroes. We invited everyone we knew who had a strong and venturesome palate, and encouraged them to invite anyone they knew who was similarly endowed. We made as much room as we could in our living and dining rooms, and put out bear loins and boar loins and hams, pickled walnuts, Wild Cherry Jelly and a vat of mulled wine punch.

The meal was a bombardment of strong flavors, an assault of wild pungent tastes on our palates. After the grave, heavy taste of the bear, a sharp jab of pickled walnut revived taste buds for the strong double-hickoried pork, whose superb gaminess melded into the smooth tartness of Wild Cherry Jelly and was quenched and stilled in the hot, spicy mulled wine. The wild strength of the food recalled the wild strength of the boar and bear, as we recalled the hunt from which the feast had come.

Feasting on Boar and Bear

Smoked Roast Russian Boar

1 wild boar
60 pounds coarse salt
Water
2 quarts bacon drippings
1 gallon ginger ale
2 pounds brown sugar

Prepare brine solution by adding 10 pounds of salt to huge barrel of cold water. Soak boar for 24 hours, changing brine every 4 hours.

Combine bacon drippings, ginger ale and brown sugar. Reserve for basting.

Build fire in large pit. Skewer boar on greenwood and suspend over forked green dogwood tree trunks.

Roast upside down for 6 hours, basting every ½ hour with prepared mixture. Turn hog upright and roast for 8 hours, basting as frequently as practical.

Keep heat moderate by adding fresh logs as required—about 50 very large hickory logs will be needed.

Remove boar from spit. Smoke for 48 hours (see page 39 for smoking instructions).

To serve cold: Slice and serve with Horseradish Cream Sauce.

To serve hot: Stud ham with cloves and heat in 325-degree oven for 1½ hours. Baste frequently with mixture of equal parts ginger ale and brown sugar.

Roast Loin of Bear

Bear loin, 8 pounds (marinated in Basic Game Marinade for 7 days)
½ pound larding pork cut into strips
½ cup butter
½ cup finely chopped onions
½ cup finely chopped carrots
½ cup finely chopped celery
8 shallots, finely chopped
2 cloves garlic, minced
12 peppercorns, crushed
1 bay leaf
1 bottle red wine
2 cups sour cream

Lard bear loin with strips of pork. Melt butter in large roasting pan and sauté vegetables until tender. Add peppercorns and bay leaf and place bear loin on top of vegetables in pan. Sear in hot oven (425 degrees) for 15 minutes.

Reduce heat to 350 degrees and roast meat for 2 hours, basting frequently with wine and pan drippings. Remove bear loin to heated platter; keep hot. Add remaining wine to pan drippings and cook mixture over high heat until it reduces by half. Put sauce through fine sieve, pressing with wooden spoon to extract purée of vegetables. Return sauce to heat and bring to boil. Blend several spoonfuls of sauce with sour cream in separate bowl, add salt.

Slowly blend sour cream into sauce and continue to simmer for 2 to 3 minutes. Add salt and pepper to taste and pour half of sauce over meat. Serve remainder in heated sauce boat.

Chapter 5.
Enticing a Wild Turkey

The turkey hunt is a test of wits, and the birds were winning. We had stalked and called and waited for two days without even seeing a gobbler. They were there and we knew it, for wild turkeys, though wary, are very indiscreet. Their scratch marks and feathers were everywhere, and their calls, perhaps critical jibes at our efforts, overwhelmed the other noises of the quiet woods.

We were hunting in the big timber, among the massive trees required to sustain the mighty weight and majestic spirit of the birds. Their roosts are in the highest, broadest trees, high up on the mountains so that in sleep these birds which walk more than they fly attain a height beyond most flying things. The thermal riding birds soar farther up into the sky, migrating geese glide overhead at many times a turkey's wildest dream of altitude, and yet at night, upon his lofty perch, the proud turkey is the highest bird of all.

The gobbler is very difficult game, and hunting him successfully requires an understanding of his character and characteristics. He is a creature of the wilderness, the virgin forest or deep swamp. And he is deeply rooted to his own personal bit of that wilderness. If something drives him from his home, he will return when conditions revert to his liking, even if he has been away for years. He fears people more than any other game animal or bird does.

The noises of civilization drive him deeper into wilderness. One sight of man and he will hide for days. He is gregarious, and rarely without the company of his kind. Flocks may consist of a tom and his harem, a hen and her offspring or even bachelor males banded together, but there is always a group of some sort, and the group always has a sentry. One sign of trouble and these incredibly suspicious birds all disappear.

Every facet of the frontiersman personality of the turkey must be known and understood to hunt him successfully, but the one that was taxing us most, even more than the wariness that had, thus far, prevented not only a shot, but even a sighting, was the pride that prompted him to roost at the very top of a mountain. Each day we stalked up to the roosting ground in a heavy stand of pine atop a mountain. Long before first light we dressed in camouflage and inched our way up to the crest, our careful path at least three miles of quiet, concealed walking. As we reached the ridge line we would crawl across, then partway down the other side to intercept the turkeys' daily stroll to luncheon in the valley. By the time we were well concealed and waiting behind a recent deadfall or a giant pine our legs would be trembling with the efforts of the stalk. The swift and silent climb claimed more than the breath we had, so that it seemed the first half hour on the stand was spent in breathing in enough to balance out the deficit. And each time the birds slipped by, our first awareness of them coming from their gobbling conversations halfway down the mountain.

We'd hunt the field below all day, but without much hope, since just one sight of us would drive the flock away, and preventing that sighting meant using caution that prevented luck as well. And then at dusk we stalked back up the mountain to try again to intercept and ambush.

Each sit was absolutely still. Unlike the deer with which they share their range wild turkeys notice form as well as motion, and so a screen of pine boughs or a log would shield us, camouflage and all. Bill called with a wooden striker on the evening sits (the return-to-roost call that he made would be unnatural in the morning and might frighten off the birds, and it was too late in the year to lure in single toms with a mating call), and voices answered but the birds never came. It almost seemed the answers were invitations for the strange caller to prove his genuineness by flying out to them.

And so we sat, our hunt carefully rehearsed. Shoot birds with beards—the males—but not too-long beards, since the length is proportional to age, and age proportional to toughness. Only hope, not reason, kept us watching the hill waiting for game, with none of the tingling alertness that comes with the expectation of a catch. We sat in silence, watching hills beyond our hill, and drifting patterns in the sky beyond them, our minds drifting, too, to formless, random thoughts that masked the thought that we would fail. It seemed we climbed and crept for this: to sit stock-still beneath a pine and see the autumn mountains through green needled blinds.

At dark, the day's hunting done, we were exhausted. For ten tense hours we had crept over the forest carpet of crisp, newfallen leaves, placing each step so carefully that no leaf announced our coming. And half those careful steps were up the sides of mountains. The other half were just as hard, for coming down we had to make sure that we weren't seen, and hold our speed with tired legs. Our concentration could not lapse at all. We always had to be concealed, to make no noise, to keep from tipping off the birds. Our arms were exhausted too, laden the day long with the heavy guns. Added to my concentration on quiet and concealment was the constant self-reminder: "Safety on. Point at the ground. Don't swing toward Bill."

Two days left us depleted. We had found feathers and droppings under the evergreens, seen scratched-up spots in the field below and heard the calling of our quarry, but hadn't seen a turkey.

Bill didn't seem disturbed. He said most hunters never find a flock, and those that do often scare them off as soon as they make contact. We were doing well to have been around for two whole days and not have spooked our prey. But still it seemed that our hard climbs should be yielding more than vistas of the changing season seen through a screen of evergreen.

The third day we decided to forget the hill and try an ambush in the field below. We got there before dawn—after first light the turkeys would see us creeping through the grass—and through the dark we found our way to a place near the bare spot where the big birds dust-bathed every noon. Bill lay down in the dew-wet grass, and I picked my stand fifty feet away.

I got as comfortable as I could, for we would have to lie like this till noon. A tuft of grass became a pillow, and I dropped off to sleep. I woke to pink streaked sky that turned the yellow stalks around me rose, and watched them turn to yellow as the sky turned blue. Grass and sky were all I saw; I watched the clumps around me sway and listened to the wind. Then on the wind there came another sound—a clear first call of turkeys feeding on the mountain, perhaps half a mile away.

The sun rose higher, till it struck my eyes, its brightness washing out the colors of the sky and grass. I lay and listened for three hours more. The wind, a chafe of grass, and now and then a feeding gobble, always closer. Near noon I heard Bill sound just once the call we'd heard the turkeys use when frolicking in the dust; he called once again ten minutes later.

I checked my shotgun—action closed, ready to shoot as soon as I clicked the safety off.

64

The timeless tedium of the wait began to be diluted by a tingle of anticipation that was missing in our forest stands. Perhaps they'll come. They're getting closer. Don't move. Keep still. Don't give the trap away. The random daydreams that filled the hours of straight, blank staring at the sky, of watching clouds move from the limit of my vision at the top of the grass at my feet to the limit of my vision at the bottom of the visor of my cap, gave way to strained listening and strong willing that the careful birds would come, would be true to their habitual natures while relaxing their deep caution. We'd left no mark upon the field, Bill would not smoke, we did not move. There was no reason for the flock to stay away. Our scent was there, of course, but local hunters had assured us that wild turkeys rely on sight and sound and, though quite wary, will ignore the strongest warnings of their sense of smell.

I heard Bill call again, but now off to my right. Then once more, softly. How did he move? And why? And then I knew our game was there. I froze and listened, straining for stillness and to hear each hint of sound that could give away the turkeys' spot.

The sounds were to my right—I was between Bill and the birds. I listened to each cluck and gobble till I heard the beating wings that meant a dust bath had begun. I clicked the safety off and

As I swung up he called out three sharp sounds and all around me the muffled-sharp slap of beating wings filled the air.

*When the logs
are smoking
well, we hang
the turkey from
one of the rods
and keep the
wood smoldering
for two days.*

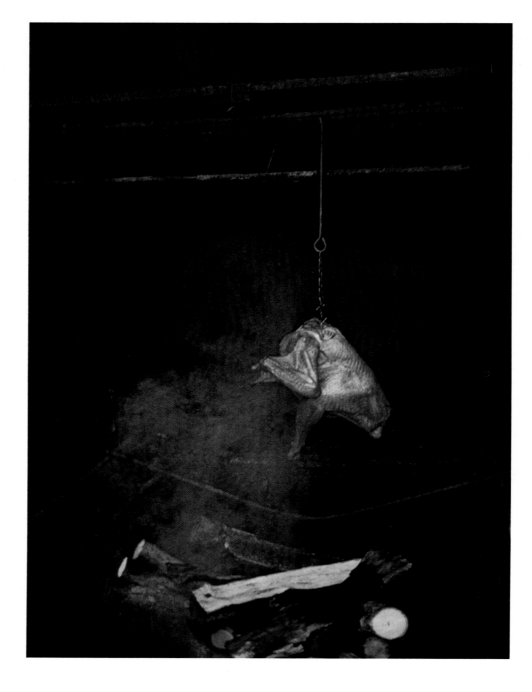

jumped up—the nearest bird was less than ten yards off. As I swung up he called out three sharp sounds and all around me the muffled-sharp slap of beating wings and the sheen of iridescent black bodies filled the air.

I picked one with a long black beard, swung, lead on his head, and shot. He crumpled and the big body crashed to the ground as I heard Bill beside me whooping out his glee.

He did not shoot; one bird would fill our needs, and we had met the challenge in the fruitful wait—the shot itself was an anticlimax. The lumbering flight of the first few wingbeats was slow enough for me to pick my target by his beard—long enough to be big, not so long as to be old and tough—and then aim at the head to keep the meat free of shot.

The flock was out of sight by the time we reached the prize. Bill hefted him and his plumage was a vibrating spectrum of reflected sun. Although his feathers were black they were of such a high gloss that each feather seemed a facet of a gemstone, and each danced back a different sparkling color, each feather's color changing with the slightest move.

The bird was more than a yard from beak to square-cut tail, and weighed at least twenty pounds. We emptied our guns and Bill slung the gobbler over his shoulder for the long walk back. Now the hike that had been such a trial was like a pleasant stroll, since cover and quiet were no longer necessary.

We cut a six-inch slit in the base of the bird's abdomen and gutted him, then hung him in his plumage for a week. After that week those lovely feathers had to come off, a hard-won fistful at a time. At last the carcass was clean and we could start the process that turns the wild, nutty flesh into a rare blending of woodland tastes. The bird was set to soak in brine while we stoked up the smokehouse.

Our smokehouse had once been a toolshed on a nearby farm, but as the land was sold off for house lots, the farm had little need of tools. We bought the old shack and had it moved to our country place. We set it over a yard-deep pit and have smoked our own game ever since. The old cedar shingles of the shack seem to lend an extra pungency to the essence of hickory and cherry that permeates our smoked meats.

To start our smoking we lay a bed of charcoal on the bottom of the pit. When it is glowing red we add green hickory or cherry logs. The logs must smolder, but not flame. More charcoal is added at the start, until the logs themselves are coals to keep their successors smoldering. When the logs are smoking well, we hang the turkey from one of the rods that span the house and keep the wood smoldering for two days.

Our care and patience in tending the fire reflects the care and patience of the hunt itself, and adds the final perfecting touch to the hunt's prize. The rich smoked turkey is a return to tastes of earlier times, too pungent, often, for palates of today. But we find the ancient taste superb, and more, a haunting evocation of the ancient methods of the turkey hunt.

Feasting on Wild Turkey

66   **Smoked Wild Turkey**

1 wild turkey (hung for 5 days)
4 cups brown sugar
4 cups coarse salt
20 cloves
8 gallons cold water

Pluck and singe the turkey.

Prepare brine of brown sugar, coarse salt, cloves and water in large earthen or stone crock.

Keep turkey in brine for 3 days.

Proceed as with Smoked Pheasant (p. 39) but increase smoking time to 48 hours.

Chapter 6.

Wild Duck in Honey

Surrounded by flickering deep orange and pale blue flames is a brace of golden ducks, the gold of their honey-roasted skin gilded by their flaming honey sauce. They rest on a silver platter, now vermeiled in the honeyed light, whose fading luminescence is more quietly restated by the flames of candles whose ornate candlesticks share with silver service the last rich aura of the dying light. The pale, soft globe of light encompasses us all, Bill, me and our guests, as we share in the pleasures of the wild duck feast. The opulence and warmth antithesize and recall the spartan cold, two weeks before this festive day, in which the feast began.

Bright purple patches daubed on burnt cork were the only color in that leaden day. All else was black or white or grey, as if all pigment had been frozen out, and only basic shapes remained. Constantly repeating volleys of sleet stung our faces in the blind. The pond still flowed, though ice-rimmed at its edges, its water drab grey in reflection of the sky. Only a strong-moving current from a spring prevented ice from closing down the pond to ducks, as the cold that seemed to fragment us into a hundred individually shivering spots was more than enough to freeze it over.

We huddled there as morning changed to afternoon in a constant grey light, no drier and no less cold as the hours of motionless vigil crept on. Icicles fringed my parka hood, and frozen sleet became white crystal baubles embroidered in the grey seal of my clothes. Bill, too, had been bejeweled with sparkling tokens of the frozen day.

The Labrador beside us seemed unaware of the discomforts of our wait, and sat with stoic patience, moving not an ear or paw, not turning his head from its fixed stare ahead. His stillness was a discipline. A frolicking or fidgeting dog would warn away the ducks, so good retrievers are trained to control all impulses toward unnecessary movement. Our stillness came from the cold. At times I thought we'd sit like blocks till spring.

Our seat was a huge felled tree trunk, surrounded by a four-foot screen of reeds. The natural blind was excellent, so we hadn't bothered with the cattail-stuffed webbing rolled in the trunk of the car. The reeds were high in back yet low enough on the pond side to give a clear field of fire at incoming birds.

We had set a raft of black duck decoys out fifty feet upwind of the stretch of water commanded by our field of fire. Ducks always land upwind and toward the stool, so they would just be putting on the brakes as they streaked by our stand. Brown earth-tone twine ran down to hemispheres of lead, each length attached to a decoy and each about five times the water's depth.

We carved the decoys of our raft ourselves, to the pattern of some that were done nearby seventy years ago. By that time local styles and conventions had been well established in all the main duck-hunting areas, and the cork-bodied birds traditional around Long Island's Great South Bay are still the best choice for the conditions here. When we hunt other areas we use native decoys whenever we can. Almost invariably the experience and experimentation of the carvers who worked during the great waterfowling era between the Civil War and the First World War had perfected the optimum decoy for the particular circumstances of each area. Ducks will sometimes come in to decoys that bear only a very stylized resemblance to waterfowl. Folded cardboard, old tires, piles of mud and tufts of grass all occasionally work. But natural selection, working over the thousand years since the Indians learned to set out painted bundles of reeds as stools, has resulted in a generally sophisticated duck population that isn't easily fooled. Although the strong flocking instinct on which the decoy

idea is based is not species-specific, and ducks will come down to
rafts of almost any sort of waterfowl, decoys should be as accurate
in counterfeiting the look of one particular species as possible.
They need not be replicas of living ducks, but should give an exact
visual impression of the species. And so, though the cork stools
that rode the wavelets of the pond were half again life size, for
better visibility, each bore a purple parallelogram on each side,
the exact purple of the speculum of the living ducks.

The cold, damp misery of the blind seemed to soak into our bones
while the chill cut through our bodies. But the discomfort of the
cold was diluted by the never spoken but always felt mood of
frozen duck stands, the shared awareness of the rigors of our
mutual quest, and the feeling of our mutual purposes, of challenges overcome and game for our table.

There are conversations, but they are wordless. "What a foul
day," and "fine for fowl," Bill's horrible pun on my misgivings
about the weather voiced earlier in the car, now is recalled in an
exchange of silly grins. And silly grins become expectant smiles
as we reflect that, pun though it is, Bill's observation is true. On
a rainy, windy day like this the ducks fly low and land often. The
need for stillness and for silence renews our resolve. Most of all
we trade wordless questions. "What was that?" at a fast low gull.
"Will they come across the trees, or from behind and circle over?"
"What did I hear?"

And finally we did hear the whistling sound of low-flying ducks.
Five whizzed by overhead. Three flashed with vivid colors—green
and brown and white and black and grey, all bright with the
ducks' vitality, even the grey vibrant by contrast with the grey
lifeless day.

We held our breath and watched and waited. The ducks streaked
past the trees beyond the pond, and every ounce of energy saved
in hours of waiting was spent now in simple will, thinking and
forcing the ducks to turn. They banked and circled, downstream
now, beyond the far end of the pond.

Only straining, circling eyes and the quiet click of safeties revealed
our wild interest. The dog made no move, but the floppy lump of
black fur had lost its shapelessness and become a clearly defined
mass of hard tensed muscle, ready to leap at the first explosion.

The ducks came over the end of the pond gliding, and we picked our shots. We waited two hour-long seconds as they came in, wings spread and braked—then up, swing, squeeze. And two dull barks exploded the quiet grey air, and the warmth of our excitement burst over our bodies.

The splash came as we shot, and by the time our guns were down the dog was halfway to the first downed duck. He swam like a clumsy sea dragon, pushing through the water in leaps, head high on each forward plunge to make sure the quarry hadn't moved. The swim back was a smooth, fast dogpaddle, the bird in the Labrador's mouth making scouting superfluous. As soon as Bill's hand had touched the duck the dog was back in the water, his wake churning waves the width of the pond, the white of his bow wave imposing its foamy vitality on the dead grey water.

Then once again we sat to wait. During the retrieves Bill had whispered that the day was like a day he had spent many years before on a pond much like this, which ended in one of nature's most thrilling displays. This dismal day, this kind of flowing pond fringed with ice, this time of year, all were pieces of a mysterious pattern whose completion meant a frenzy of ducks converging on the pond from all sides just before sunset.

And they came—pitching, swirling, tumbling down in a wildly darting torrent over the trees. Sixes, tens, twenties—blacks and mallards in straight, fast trajectories, each path marked by a blur of motion, a splash of color, all moving, from all angles, their speed and recrossing paths forming wild, kinetic, abstract tracing on the sky and on our minds. Our eyes, seeming to surpass the farthest limits of normal vision, registered every nuance of this devil's dance of ducks, seeing both the pattern whole and each pinfeather of that pattern's every part.

We held our crouch, we held our fire, the watching of this weird cascading gathering rite more important than the game. When the last duck had settled, the pond was blanketed by their feathery backs. Blacks and mallards shared the pond with our twenty cork imposters. There was no room for them to move about. Each duck was packed tight against its neighbor. The dull-brown mallard ducks and dark-brown backs of blacks were interspersed with the emerald flashes of the drake mallards' heads.

*We had
our limit.
Four
beautiful
mallards.*

The birds are drenched with a honeyed sauce, and then anointed with a soupçon of fine Cognac.

We simply looked at the crowded pond for several minutes, then Bill stood up and waved his handkerchief above his head, and the sky all around us was filled with escaping ducks. We waited a moment, then each bagged one more duck. The sound of the shots restored order to the world of the dog, who had sat in stupefied confusion as the vast flock gathered. He splashed into action, we unloaded our guns, and then we were on the way home. We had the limit, four beautiful mallards. As the car's heater thawed us we started to plan the feast, two weeks away.

The birds were gutted through a slit at the base of the abdomen, then hung in plumage for five days. After the aging outside our window (we had not had to refrigerate the ducks for the temperature never went above 36 degrees), the birds were brought in and stripped of their feathers by being dunked in hot paraffin, cooled and peeled.

Then they went into a great stone crock to marinate. After five days of absorbing the subtle flavors of wine, oil and herbs, they were ready for the feast.

The mallards are served with elegant wild rice, which is itself the fruit of a successful hunt. Each year in Minnesota the Chippewas pursue the rice as we pursued the game. A treaty gives them the sole right to harvest the purple grain from the grasses of their swamps. One man poles each ricing boat through the man-high plants, while another flails each clump of green enough to spray the purple grain into the boat. They have a season, ricing wardens, and the feeling of the hunt about their work. Their hard-won harvest has always seemed the only fitting complement to the hard-won harvests of our duck hunts.

The preparations for the feast are as much a ritual as the hunt itself. In the morning I cover a cup of rinsed wild rice with boiling water and set it aside to cool. Throughout the day I will drain and repeat the process until, at last, each grain has puffed and swelled to its full bloom.

I take the birds carefully out of their stone crocks and wipe them inside and out with a dry cloth. Then I peel the outer skin of a navel orange, bruising the rind to release the fine, tart oils, and rub the marinated birds with it. Next I rub the outside of each bird slowly and gently with a mixture of herbs and seasonings until the aromatic blend covers the birds as lightly and completely as mist.

Next I blend the honey sauce, stirring gently as the ingredients mingle in the wooden spoon's slow swirling path, and rub the cavity of each bird with its exotic sweetness. I make a sauce of the sweet remnants in the roasting pan. The birds are drenched with that honied sauce, and then anointed with a soupçon of fine cognac. The touch of a match to matchless liquor, and the flames burst to life. Their warmth and magic captivates us all, until in fading, they relinquish their captives to Bill who starts to carve the honied ducks and begins the tale of the hunt.

Feasting on Wild Duck

Wild ducks must be hung in plumage for 5 days and marinated in Basic Game Marinade for 5 days. Follow same procedure as with Canada goose in eviscerating, hanging, marinating and plucking.

Wild Duck in Honey

2 mallard ducks (hung in plumage and marinated)
4 teaspoons salt
2 teaspoons ground ginger
2 teaspoons dried and powdered basil
1 teaspoon pepper
2 cups honey
½ cup butter
¼ cup orange juice
3 teaspoons lemon juice
2 teaspoons grated orange peel
¼ teaspoon dry mustard
2 oranges
2 teaspoons potato flour
4 tablespoons cognac

Remove birds from marinade and dry thoroughly inside and out. Combine salt, ginger, basil and pepper. Rub half of mixture inside duck.

Heat honey, butter, orange juice, lemon juice, orange peel, mustard and a pinch of salt in double boiler.

Rub 3 tablespoons of this mixture inside each duck.

Slice each orange, with skin, into 6 wedges. Stuff ducks with as many as possible.

Pour 4 more tablespoons of honey mixture into ducks, and truss the ducks.

Rub remaining basil mixture on outside of duck.

Place each duck on large sheet of aluminum foil.

Pour honey mixture over each bird, wrap securely and roast in a slow oven (325 degrees) for 2 hours.

Unwrap. Baste ducks with drippings and roast 30 minutes more, basting frequently. Place ducks on heated platter.

Combine potato flour with a little cold water. Add to honey mixture, stir and heat to boiling. Serve in heated sauce boat.

Pour heated cognac over ducks, ignite and present to guests.

Wild Rice with Wild Cherry Jelly

1 cup wild rice
2 tablespoons butter
2 tablespoons Wild Cherry Jelly
1 tablespoon red wine
Salt
Freshly ground black pepper

Place the wild rice in strainer and wash thoroughly with cold water.

Drain and place in pan deep enough for water to extend at least 1 inch over rice.

Cover with boiling water and let stand until water cools.

Drain, and repeat this procedure 4 times, adding 1 level teaspoon salt to the last boiling water, and let rice open completely.

When open, drain thoroughly.

Melt butter in heavy skillet.

Add Wild Cherry Jelly and wine and allow to melt slowly. Fold in rice, stirring carefully with wooden spoon.

Add salt and pepper to taste. Cook about 5 minutes over low heat, stirring constantly.

Mallard Duck à la Presse

2 mallard ducks, hung and marinated
4 tablespoons cognac
1 cup red wine
6 tablespoons butter
2 mashed duck livers (2 tablespoons)
2 tablespoons Wild Cherry Jelly
4 tablespoons pâté de foie gras
1 tablespoon lemon juice
½ teaspoon allspice

The Catch
And
The Feast

Remove ducks from Basic Game Marinade and pat dry.

Rub them inside and out with cognac and salt and pepper.

Roast birds in very hot oven (475 degrees) for 15 minutes.

Carve off breasts and place them in chafing dish with blood reserved from carving.

Cover chafing dish and turn on flame.

Place duck carcasses and all drippings in duck press.

Combine red wine, butter, lightly sautéed mashed duck livers, Wild Cherry Jelly, pâté de foie gras, lemon juice and allspice.

Pour into duck press. Turn wheel to force pressings into warmed bowl.

Strain sauce. Pour over duck breasts in chafing dish.

Stir in cognac and ignite.

Serve on hot plates with Wild Rice with Wild Cherry Jelly.

74

Chapter 7.

Mixed Bag of Small Game

The pennant of the small game hunt is a white flag—not of surrender, but of pursuit. It is carried high, on the tip of the straight-stretched tail of a beagle working in the brush. Those two or three inches of white fur are as important to the hunt as the dog's nose, since the catch is virtually guaranteed, and watching the hounds at work is the primary pleasure of the day.

Two flags are fluttering now, two white-waving, eye-grabbing spots above the dry grass that hides all other trace of dogs. They move in bursts. Ten feet, and then a turn. Twenty feet, then circle back. Quick darts, and slower careful checks, crossing and recrossing as they quarter the field sniffing out the first fresh trace of game. Bill and I amble down the path next to the field, nothing to do now but watch. The field grass is the bright gold that shines before the winter brown, shimmering in brighter ripples that follow the paths of the dogs. Bushes form black skeleton patterns against the gold, their leaves now brown on the dull-brown ground. Their tracery is mirrored in the black trunks and branches of the trees across the field, whose still-clinging leaves are a pale yellow reflection of the gold-yellow grass. The cold fall brightness intensifies contrast, so that trees and bushes and shadows are drawn in the same black ink, while grass and leaves become solid elements of a graphic design; yet it also so intensifies detail that each stalk and twig of the vast pattern leaps forward with an exaggerated depth dimensionality that separates and isolates it from each other stalk and twig in the panoramic composition.

Although we can only see their tails we know exactly what the dogs are doing. They are trotting back and forth through the grass with noses to the ground, each sniffing breath a check for recent game. The younger dog, well trained but still learning, looks up from time to time. His teacher and model doesn't waste the effort. He is a scent hound, not a courser. His years in the field have taught him that his nose is his most effective tool—and that a rabbit that can camouflage itself to near invisibility with its stillness cannot camouflage its scent.

A waving tail stiffens and there is a howl, and sympathetic barking from the dog not yet on the scent. Then a second howl starts as both dogs work the trail. Bill watches the dogs as I watch the path. The rabbit will be well ahead of the hounds, and if we both watched only them, we'd never see the game. "They're moving straight down the field, about twenty feet in," Bill advises. I hear the hounds' music, still off to the right, as I see a grey blur streak across the trail, and see a small steel bead over the center of it, the bead of my shotgun, up and shot reflexively.

I click on the safety as reflex, then walk up to the rabbit. The dogs are there, but they've lost interest. The game is dead, their job is done. They wait in impatient respite for the next hunt to begin while Bill and I admire the catch. The supple shape is masked by soft grey-brown fur, pure white on chest and belly and puff of tail. A patch of deep red that marks the clean head shot is the only color.

"Good shot," says Bill, but not much more. Small game is more a harvest than a hunt, and the vital excitement of the chase is replaced here with the enjoyment of the day itself and the quiet satisfaction of collecting good things to eat. The dogs both get a pat and thanks, in happy, admiring voices they can understand, even if they do not know the words. Then the wagging tails of their joy in our appreciation become the wagging tails of work as the hunt goes on.

We watch the flags again, and watch the field, but just to see it, not to see the game. We might find more if we went through the grass to flush the rabbits out, but the dogs will find enough to fill our needs. My gun is lighter now, as hunting guns all are after they have brought down food. It's still a gun, and still I check the safety often, but now it is a partner in a good pursuit, not a heavy dead weight as guns often seem in the first half hour when it's possible that there will be no game.

We talk the talk of the field as we walk along a little behind the dogs. Our hunting jackets and hats are vital for safety, but the heavy trousers and boots are only worn from habit on a cool dry day like this. Our guns are loaded, safeties on, and pointed at the ground. The chokes are fairly tight, for better, cleaner shots at rabbit, possible at longer distances than with birds. The talk comes in small islands of words in the quiet sea of tiny sounds of the field, as we watch the sea of field grass ripple in the wake of the scurrying dogs.

The young dog howls, then starts to run, running past a turn in the rabbit's trail. He is perplexed to find the scent gone, but his mentor, trailing at a brisk trot, is there and is not fooled. Our guns stay down, for the dogs are moving away from us. This rabbit will range far, and we climb a little rise on the far side of the path to watch. From here we can see black patches of back beneath the white tail tips as the hounds dart forward, stop, circle, then move again. The circling is at the spots where the rabbit stopped or turned, and the dogs are silent, concentrating on sniffing out the new direction. But on the sprints the hounds give voice, their music flying to us like peals of living bells. The baying is more excited now, the interruptions less frequent, as the dogs come closer to their prey. The closeness is in time rather than distance. The rabbit might have had five minutes' lead when first they got the scent. He now has two. The distance between them is still quite short—the dogs' trotting pace and circling and the rabbit's favorite defense of absolute stillness might make those minutes into a hundred yards or less.

The pace picks up—the sprints are longer now, as fear drives the quarry farther between his stops. The skirmishing is almost over and the chase about to begin. The trail is unbroken now and the dogs are at a slow run. We are delighted to see the young hound leave the trail and swing out to one side to try to turn the rabbit toward us. The peals are now a steady song, the full round bark of the tracking dog seconded by those of the flanker, whose adolescent voice still cracks on the heady music of the hunt.

They chase into the trees bordering the field and disappear, but still the music comes. The sound seems like sweet shafts that pierce the air in hard, straight lines, and though they are out of sight, we can tell the dogs' positions as easily as we could by watching the waving of their white-tipped tails. They cross a hill and the sound is muffled now, but still we can hear the direction. They are turning.

We listen to a semicircle of sounds as the flanker does his job and heads the quarry back to us. When they come out of the woods the dogs are in tandem again. No need for turning now; they run straight toward our knoll. Bill watches along the path while I watch the dogs and call out every change of direction. Then I hear the harsh, flat sound beside me as Bill fires, then fires again so fast it seems one prolonged noise. We check our safeties and go down. The rabbit lies where we were standing when the chase began. This time the dogs get more than pats. We open up the sandwiches we carry and give each one a slice of meat as a reward, then pat them and talk long in approving voices. The talk will be even longer tonight, when we return them to their owner and tell him of the young dog's progress.

The hunt has left both beagles tired. At the end they had spotted the rabbit and started coursing, running at full speed since scenting was not necessary. We walk toward the woods beyond the rise, not hunting now, just strolling to the next spot. The dogs are content to walk beside us, panting.

The panting stops fifty feet from the trees, then the sound returns. But now it's sniffing, as the dogs, rested, begin to hunt the grass between us and the next hunting place.

The trees are thin and scattered here, the little woods not much more than an overgrown meadow. The dogs work differently in the thicker brush that surrounds the occasional maples. They sniff and flush, trying to detect game and making enough commotion while they're about it to frighten out any that might be hiding. Bill and I follow more closely now, watching the ground ahead for a rabbit making a sudden break. Any shot we get will be unexpected, just as the game flushes from cover, with at most a bark or two from the dogs to announce the opportunity.

The dogs seem to be even more pleased to be hunting in the woods than in the field. They love to add the bluster of a rush into a bush to drive out game to the more serious business of sniffing for it, and the show they put on makes it hard to remember to watch the ground ahead for targets. They rustle through the few fallen leaves as if they are a pack, and seem to be a pack as their forays under bushes and scenting explorations of the ground multiply them, now teaming up, now independent.

The young dog trots into a bush and there is an explosion, an explosion sustained as a ruffed grouse rises on my right. I swing, lead, shoot—but no shot fires. Bill's gun goes off beside me, then again as I click my safety off, but the bird is gone in a brown blur of heavy beating wings. It seems that even the beagles' eyes are bulging with the shock of the grouse, and it takes a minute or two for the four of us to get back to hunting.

We start again, the dogs a pack in their magnified noises and "everywhere-at-once" scurrying, Bill and I a regiment with the leaves rustling multiplication of every step. Our sounds are all around us in the woods, as if the autumn smell in the air here diffuses the noises that had such clear directionality in the field below. There is a frenzied scattering of leaves as a rabbit bursts from a bush. Again my shot is off before I know my gun is up, and Bill shoots with me.

Ten paces to collect the kill, two pats for dogs, and we move on. The trees come thicker now, and from them bursts another grouse. This time he veers toward Bill, and that mistake means grouse for our small game feast. The bird is a plump one, smaller than a pheasant, but fuller breasted and fuller feathered, in a dull downy brown flecked with black that makes him all but invisible until he surges into the air.

A sweep of one more field, and two more rabbits complete this segment of the small game hunt. We have the makings of a tremendous rabbit dinner and a bonus supper of grouse for two.

Bill wears rubber gloves to clean the rabbits, and each liver is carefully examined for the white spots that signal tuleremia. The disease is rare, but it does exist, so the precaution of keeping the blood from touching him (since it might get into some tiny nick or cut) is worthwhile; we have never found the telltale spots.

After gutting and salting, the grouse and rabbits are hung in the shade for a week. If the temperature goes above 36 degrees the game must be hung in a refrigerator. After aging both are marinated for five days, then are ready to cook or freeze.

Rabbit can be the simplest, plainest sort of food, or a truly noble dish. The marinade is the first step in the ennobling process. The second is the sauce. We cut the carcasses into portions, forelegs, hind legs and segments of loin, and wrap each segment in a thin strip of bacon with chunks of butter. Then we bake them for an hour and a half in a sour cream sauce that is the perfect complement to its countrified nature. The result is a meal one might well be served in an elegant villa, château, dascha or country house— universal in its excellence, elegance and easy availability.

The relaxed stroll of the rabbit hunt has its converse in the high-tension stalk of the quail. Whether they burst from cover before being detected or in front of a pointing dog, bobwhites always take me by surprise.

We hunt quail in the fields around our country place, big, open fields, planted in berries, grain or clover, now harvested but still lush feeding places for quail. I had passed these fields for years, and even hunted them for goose, and never knew the quail were there. The shy birds stay under the ground cover, and only a dog or a very lucky and deliberate hunter can get them out and up. Our dog is a neighbor's house pet who happened to be a regular summer visitor—perhaps because of the steakbones Bill saved for him—and, who during the course of his visits, seemed to be learning the rudiments of his birthright craft. Each fall he looks a little plump, and we, as good neighbors, volunteer to let him come along on some of our walks to get a little exercise. He takes to the field deep in steakbone debt, but always repays each feast he has enjoyed with a quail feast for us, and always with some interest. It seems that just his presence is enough to send up quail that would sit tight if Bill or I alone stepped on their tails. He prances into green rye grass and before he can take a point a covey will shoot up like a geyser of quicksilver, the explosive sound of beating wings louder than the explosions of our guns. The first covey never yields a quail, but just prepares us all for the morning's task.

I stop admiring the bright green of the rye in the drab brown late autumn world, and remind myself to watch the bird I plan to shoot and not the scattered shotgun pattern of the birds in flight. The Labrador recalls his function and resolves to wind the next batch to us instead of trotting up to investigate the scent that seemed to call to some centuries-old instinct in his blood. Bill merely laughs, and then points out the singles he has watched instead of shooting at the scattering flock. In this case watching is more productive than shooting, for he knows that, surprised, he will down, at best, one bird and I won't even shoot. By following the birds to their next roost, we can take four from the broken covey.

Bill points the dog toward the nearest hiding bird and I walk up, gun ready, behind the point. When I am set Bill sends the dog ahead and a projectile launches out of the rye. My gun is up and I shoot fast. In four or five seconds the bird will land again and run along under the cover till safely out of range. I swing the shotgun's bead past the blurred streak and touch off one, keep swinging and fire another if I missed.

Bill takes the next, then I, then Bill again, until we've taken four from the covey. Bill connects with every second bird, I with every fourth I try, for though I'm always sure I lead enough, quail fly at fifty miles per hour and accelerate to that speed quickly, so enough lead when I pull the trigger might not be enough when the shot is out at the distance of the target. When four round birds are hanging at Bill's belt, or when the singles have all scurried off under cover, we move on. A field will often shelter several coveys and we are ready for the next.

When the dog winds the birds our guns go up, our safeties off. When Bill shouts "Flush" the Labrador's first few steps are usually enough to send a flash of black in all directions. I try to pick a bird, I try to lead, I try to keep from thinking that I must connect if I just fire into the center of the fast dispersing cloud. And still I usually miss. If one bird falls to all three shells in my gun I have done well. Bill gets one always, two on rare occasions. Then home for cleaning, a two-day aging and two days in marinade and we can count on our small game feast. The dog's feast comes at once. Bill tends to carve far from the bone when serving our traditional quail-day lunch of rare charcoal-broiled steak.

A grouse hunt is much like the hunt for quail, but flat fields give way to rugged hills in this pursuit. We may down a bird or two in hunting rabbit, but to be sure of a grouse feast we set aside one day of our deer hunting time to hunt the thicker, colder woods the grouse prefer.

Grouse tend to roost in pine trees, but I never see their bulky forms until the roar of their wings marks their departure. The first I downed was my proudest bag, the prize of my most humiliating hunt. Bill and I were stalking through a pine stand when a helicopter-rush of beaten air shocked me into immobility. By the time I whirled to shoot the bird was gone, but Bill had marked his landing spot. He pointed out the large, lone pine and I walked up, gun ready, all senses perfectly alert, determined not to be duped again. I didn't notice my split second of distraction but my quarry did, and exploded over my head. This time he landed in a stand of small pines, and when my composure returned I stalked up once again—and once again was caught in an instant of inatten-

tion. Twice more I stalked, and twice more lost the contest of concentration to the bird. Four flushes and not a shot was fired. My husband and the grouse both seemed amused. The last flight ended in a stand so thick I could not see the tree in which the grouse had landed, and as I crept through it the bird made his mistake. I passed his tree and he sat tight, but when I had gone beyond he flushed. The flight was long and I had time to whirl, to aim, to lead and to collect a delicious meal and my most prized hunting trophy. Each year we get a brace or two of grouse—no more. But those few birds are prouder prizes than the buck which is the object of our mountain trip.

The feasting is done simply and alone. No guest could appreciate the rich seasoning of accomplishment that glorifies the simply roasted bird we share.

T he only hunt whose joys I cannot seem to appreciate with Bill is the squirrel hunt. The method is simply to go into a forest and sit against a tree until the ubiquitous little creatures forget about the noise we made in arriving and resume their branch hopping. When Bill picks one off with his .22 they all retreat, and once again we sit absolutely still until their fear dispels. Another shot, another wait, repeated until Bill's game pockets contain four squirrels, enough for squirrel pie. The shooting is difficult—the target is the head, the distance usually fifty yards—but the game is always there.

Bill pretends that the right spot must be found, the right time picked, but I contend that it is impossible to sit still for fifteen minutes in *any* hardwood grove in North America and not see at least three or four squirrels. And even though the shot is hard, a miss just doesn't matter. The same squirrel will be on the same limb fifteen minutes later to offer another chance.

I pass up squirrel hunts whenever I can, and now have Bill convinced that my squirming keeps the game away, so I can pass them up often. If squirrels were not so amazingly sweet and succulent I might try to persuade Bill that my acquiescence to (and eventual eager participation in) every other form of hunting merited reciprocal consideration from him and that squirrel should be dropped from the game schedule, but his squirrel pie is so delicious that I content myself with a morning of puttering while he collects the ingredients.

Our most exotic small game pursuit is really of the commonest small game of all: blackbirds. Although grackles are a treasured delicacy in Europe they are rarely shot here. Since they are so seldom pursued, we need not bother with the elaborate decoys needed on the Continent. Our blackbird expeditions, requiring only shotguns, would be the envy of an Italian hunter whose lures include flutterings disks and dummy birds, elaborately hinged and rigged to nod their heads and flap their wings when puppet-like control strings are pulled.

We decided to try blackbird shooting after seeing and tasting the results of those complex machinations one fall we spent in Italy. Every fine restaurant and all the good butcher shops were decorated with festoons of little birds, hanging like feathered bouquets, dozens in each bunch. At first I was appalled, for the Italians consider songbirds fair game, too, and larks and sparrows were splashes of color in the glossy black field. But "When in Rome . . ." and so we were, and so we tried them.

The first taste made us converts. We made the rounds of gun shops for the decoys and got them at a bargain since it was the season's end. We got owls and crows that moved as if alive—the blackbirds' natural enemies, and their irresistible victims when a flock of grackles finds one alone. We got disks and wire and every imaginable sort of rig to duplicate the splendid blackbird feast, but we needn't have bothered.

The first time we went out a flight of grackles blotted half the sky before we got the decoys in place, and we were so busy shooting that we never did bother to put the decoys out.

The only difficulty involved in preparing "Uccelletti" comes after the hunt. Each tiny bird would seem to have as many feathers as a full-grown pheasant, and four birds are needed for each serving. We pluck for days on end, but the results are worth it. There is no more flamboyantly flavorful meal in all of our small game harvest than Uccelletti.

Although we love all our small game feasts the best of all is the finale. We freeze part of each harvest for one extravagant meal of *all* the small game dishes. Each takes on a whole new range of tastes when blended with the others. The sour of rabbit in sour cream is offset by the sweetness of the squirrel, the delicate quail followed and engulfed by pungent Uccelletti, the creamy grouse leads back to sour cream of rabbit and the cycle starts again with alternating nibbles from the wild cascade of flavors of game and sauces that seem to touch and scintillate every taste bud that we possess with the lush variety of pleasures of the meal.

Feasting on Small Game

Dressing a Rabbit

Clean rabbit immediately after the hunt. Slit it down the front, discard entrails. Sprinkle a fistful of salt inside the cavity. Hang in fur for 5 days.

Follow same hanging procedure as with pheasant.

To skin rabbit, slit fur at back legs and peel skin off like a glove. Discard head and feet. Cut rabbit into serving pieces.

Marinate in Basic Game Marinade (enough for 2 pounds of game) for 4 days.

Rabbit in Cream

1 rabbit (which has been hung and marinated)
¼ pound butter

¼ pound salt pork, thinly sliced
½ pound lean bacon, thinly sliced
4 tablespoons brandy
2 cups sour cream
Salt
Freshly ground black pepper
Chopped parsley

Remove rabbit pieces from marinade and pat dry.

Season with salt and pepper.

Place a large dab of butter on each piece and wrap 1 strip of salt pork and 2 strips of lean bacon around it.

Place in covered casserole with brandy; bake, covered, for 1¾ hours at 325 degrees.

Remove bacon and salt pork strips.

Pour off fat, leaving about four tablespoons.

Return casserole to oven, uncovered, for 20 minutes.

Put sour cream in earthen bowl, sprinkle with salt.

Add 2 tablespoons of hot drippings from casserole; blend thoroughly. (This will prevent curdling later.)

Add cream to casserole, use wooden spoon to blend in the brown crustiness.

Return to oven for 10 minutes. Cream will take on a beautiful pale orange color.

Serve from casserole. Sprinkle with chopped parsley.

Dressing a Squirrel

Follow the same procedure as for rabbit.

Squirrel Pie

2 squirrels
  (which have been hung and marinated)
6 tablespoons flour
6 tablespoons olive oil
1½ cups beef stock
2 cups red burgundy
4 sprigs parsley
2 sprigs thyme
12 medium mushrooms
½ cup salt pork, diced
12 glazed pearl onions
1 rich pastry crust
Salt
Freshly ground black pepper

Remove squirrel from marinade. Cut into serving pieces.

Dry thoroughly. Season with salt and pepper; sprinkle with flour (coat all sides).

Sauté squirrel pieces in hot olive oil. When well browned, skim fat (reserve a small quantity), add beef stock, wine, parsley and thyme.

Simmer for 1½ hours.

Brown mushrooms in reserved fat.

Sauté diced salt pork.

Remove squirrel pieces to heated dish.

Strain sauce into clean heated casserole.

Add squirrel pieces, browned mushrooms, glazed onions, sautéed diced salt pork.

Cover casserole with thick pastry crust; press firmly around rim.

Make three small slits in the middle of the crust; bake for 1 hour in a 350-degree oven.

Dressing Ruffed Grouse

86

Handle ruffed grouse as you would pheasant.

Hang for four days and marinate in Basic Game Marinade for 3 days.

Salmis of Ruffed Grouse

2 grouse (hung and marinated)
½ cup butter
1 onion, finely chopped
2 carrots, finely chopped
1 shallot, finely chopped
1 clove garlic, finely chopped
¾ cup dry white wine
2 tablespoons flour
1 cup chicken stock
1 bay leaf
2 sprigs thyme
3 sprigs parsley
2 stalks celery
4 peppercorns
12 mushroom caps
1 tablespoon lemon juice
Salt
Freshly ground pepper
Finely chopped parsley
Sautéed bread triangles

Remove grouse from marinade; pat dry.

Truss birds, spread with softened butter and roast in a 425-degree

*We have
the makings
of a
tremendous
rabbit dinner
and a
bonus supper
of grouse
for two.*

Although we love all our small game feasts the best of all is the finale—one extravagant meal of all the small game dishes.

oven for 35 minutes, basting every 5 minutes.

Remove the breasts to heated serving dish; spoon a bit of butter over them.

Set the legs and carcass aside.

Sauté finely chopped onion, carrots, shallot and garlic until golden.

Add wine and simmer, stirring constantly until liquid reduces by a third.

Add flour, stir well.

When sauce thickens, add stock, bay leaf, thyme, parsley, celery, peppercorns, salt, carcass, trimmings and juices from the birds.

Cover; simmer gently for 1 hour.

Slice the leg meat from bones and arrange with the sliced breasts.

Sauté mushroom caps in 2 tablespoons of butter and 1 tablespoon lemon juice until tender. Drain.

Strain sauce, add mushrooms and the sliced grouse; simmer for 10 minutes.

Serve on heated serving dish; garnish with triangles of bread sautéed in butter.

Sprinkle with finely chopped parsley.

Dressing Quail

Follow the same procedure for quail as for pheasant.

Reduce hanging period to 24 hours.

Marinate for 24 hours in Marinade for Small Birds.

Marinade for Small Birds

1 cup dry sherry
½ cup cognac
2 small onions, sliced
2 small carrots, sliced
4 sprigs parsley
½ teaspoon thyme

Place birds in small earthen crock.

Combine ingredients for marinade using quantities above for each 4 birds; pour over birds.

Marinate for 24 hours in cool place (not refrigerated).

Quail Baked in Butter and Wine

6 plump quail (hung and marinated)
12 tablespoons foie gras

6 truffles
¼ cup butter
6 thin strips of salt pork
1 cup dry white wine
2 tablespoons lemon juice
2 tablespoons red currant jelly
Salt
White pepper
White grapes

Remove quail from marinade; dry thoroughly.

Stuff each quail with 2 tablespoons foie gras and one truffle.

Sprinkle with salt and white pepper.

Sauté quail in ¼ pound butter in heavy-bottomed casserole, basting with frothing butter until birds are golden on all sides.

Place a strip of salt pork over the breast of each bird.

Add ½ cup wine and lemon juice.

Bake, covered, in a 350-degree oven for 35 minutes, or until they are tender.

Baste frequently.

88

Remove to heated serving dish.

Skim fat from pan.

Add ½ cup dry white wine and 2 tablespoons currant jelly; bring to a boil.

Continue cooking liquid until it thickens. Pour over quail.

Garnish with bunch of white grapes.

Uccelletti with Black Olives

24 blackbirds
   (grackles—allow 4 birds per person)
Salt and pepper
6 bruised juniper berries
½ cup cognac
¾ cup dry white wine
2 tablespoons lemon juice
2 crushed bay leaves
5 bruised peppercorns
6 tablespoons olive oil
3 tablespoons tomato paste
½ cup white stock
2 cloves garlic, crushed
12 stoned black olives
12 filleted anchovies
¾ cup strained marinade
24 sautéed bread triangles
Glass of Marsala

Clean, pluck, and singe 24 grackles. Cut off heads and feet.

Rub insides with salt and pepper and crushed juniper berry.

Place in shallow earthen dish and marinate in a mixture of cognac, ½ cup white wine, lemon juice, bay leaves, peppercorns and juniper berries for 6 hours.

Remove birds from marinade; dry thoroughly; sprinkle with salt and pepper.

Brown well on all sides in hot olive oil.

Remove birds to heated bowl; keep them warm.

Add tomato paste and stock to drippings in which birds have browned.

Add garlic, peppercorns, black olives and anchovies; stir well.

Add strained marinade and ¼ cup white wine.

Simmer for 10 minutes, then return birds to pan.

Cover and cook very gently for 1 hour or until birds are tender.

Serve birds on crisp triangles of bread sautéed in butter.

Add small wineglass of Marsala to sauce just before pouring over birds.

89

Chapter 8.

The Trout Ritual

If I were inclined to be intimidated by things complex beyond my understanding, my trout fishing experiences might still be limited to practicing roll casts on the lawn. Trout fishing is a ritual— at times it seems like a religion unto itself—and the faithful are always ready to deluge a neophyte with endless rites, customs and bits of lore. At times it seems that a proper trout fisherman, like the old English conception of a proper gentleman, took seven generations to develop.

After I had several seasons of less exalted fishing to my credit, Bill decided to telescope those seven generations into a few decades of concentrated instruction and make a trout fisherman of me. It started with several weeks of orientation. There were trips to the stream, guided tours through his tackle boxes, and endless tales of streams fished and fish hooked, each tale containing an illustrative example of some point of technique or tradition.

Bill was enjoying himself tremendously, going through equipment not used from year to year, fondling precious antique reels too fine to sully with wet line, recalling old battles won and lost in which this or that lure had been the intermediary between him and some particularly memorable trout. The gear was limitless. Dozens of boxes, each a masterpiece of exquisite wood and brass, were filled with hundreds of felt- or lamb's-wool-lined compartments containing exotic feathered assemblages in the shapes and colors of every imaginable minnow and bug—and every species was portrayed in the various shapes it assumed in every different season. A row of compartments would trace the growth of some water bug from birth to maturity, the subtle changes in size and color reflecting the passage of as little as a week in its life cycle. And the next row would be the same bug, but from a colder climate or a shadier brook or born later in the season. They were tiny fragile things, plump, yet delicate. Each was a miniature feathery jewel, and each rested luxuriantly in what seemed a jewelbox compartment, carefully fitted with the soft lining best calculated for the particular sort of feather from which it was made.

If the flies seemed jewels, the rods were like magic wands. Each was in a carefully fitted aluminum tube case and lovingly tailored chamois sleeve. They were lustrous with the rich glow of old, well-tended wood. Each rod was a handmade, hand-rubbed, seven- to nine-foot length of quivering split bamboo, whose magical appearance was reinforced by its weightlessness. They seemed to have literally no substance. Some weighed as little as an ounce and a half, none more than four ounces. As he showed me these treasures, Bill demonstrated their action—a flick of his wrist and each rod undulated in smooth waves down its spidery length. It seemed impossible that they could support their own vibrations without breaking. I couldn't imagine that a fish could be hooked and landed with one.

The reels seemed the epitome of the trout cult's love of superb impedimenta. They serve no purpose but convenient line storage, yet each was a handsome and venerable treasure. Creels and nets and even hats and waders, all seemed to be made from patterns set down eons ago and observed reverently ever since.

Every bit of this vast, yet miniature, store of equipment had one particular *proper* use. These flies were for evenings with intermittent moonlight, those for drizzling days in the second week of April. One rod was for still water, one for mountain streams in spring thaw. It all was dizzying.

Although we had observed many rituals in our pursuit of other game, the gear, at least, had always seemed tougher, bolder, more inviting to use and master quickly. The oriental complexities of the delicate tools of trout fishing seemed to prohibit any touch but one with finesse and elegance that could come only from years of cultivation.

Thre seemed to be no place to start. Then I decided to simplify. I was only interested in the secondary aspects of the sport, the quiet times together at the stream and the delicious trout those times would produce, so I would dispense with all the occult rigmarole. I would concentrate on one particular technique and just not let the other trappings intrude.

I found my métier in a corner of one of Bill's least used portfolios. There were some snips of chenille wrapped around tiny hooks and some lengths of ordinary pipe cleaner. Their colors and sizes varied, but they seemed infinitely simpler than the myriad flies I had been shown. My destiny as a fly fisherman was sealed.

"What bugs are these supposed to be?" I asked. "Wooly worms, caterpillars, little leaf bugs," Bill replied. "You fish them like nymphs. But don't worry about those now. They're really only a kind of joke." "Like nymphs" were the words that stood out, for Bill had told me that nymphs were the hardest lures to fish well. But intuition had guided me to these lures and instinct had wedded my trout fishing destiny to their tiny barbs at first sight. I wasn't about to let the fact that the way I had chosen was the hardest way dissuade me from following it. For although the fates had apparently chosen a difficult task for me, they had also given me a tool for achieving it: an idea.

The idea was simply color. I would dye, tint, paint hundreds of little lures. Since, unlike the feathers of most flies, which are used only in their natural state or dyed carefully and laboriously, my chenille could be dyed easily anywhere, I would even carry dyes as I fished, and whip up lures on the spot to match any real bugs I saw floating on the water. Bill thought I was ready to try some actual fishing, and at nine one drizzly night decided that there could be no better time for me to start. I hadn't told him of my heretic approach to trout fishing, and the mood of the evening was too pleasant to shatter with my sacrilege, so I just took a big flamboyant maribou streamer and we were off.

Bill belonged to a trout club near our country home. Their stream was like a place transplanted from another time. Tall shade trees paralleled and overhung the grassy, mossy banks. Spring water flowed fast, not splashing, but with the special heavy viscosity of the very coldest streams. But for the surface reflections, the trout seemed to be silvery projectiles that lazed, then flashed through crystalline air.

Although seeing the trout was easy, catching them was not. These were not lazy hatchery trout, but natives of the stream, several generations away from the time of the stream's stocking. Their natural food was plentiful, so the only way to catch them was to counterfeit the natural diet with flies. It was a precise duplication of a stream in the wild, except for its accessibility and longer season.

The banks were slippery that night, even though the trees kept off the rain. We started upstream enveloped in a fine mist that was full of the smell of the wet grass and leaves. The water was velvety black, a void except for the quiet gurgling and the occasional splash of a striking fish. I picked my way carefully along the bank, scudding along the fly as I went. At first I did it by feel,

but as soon as my eyes started to get accustomed to the dark, the flashy white streamer stood out, and I could watch its action as I flicked the rod tip.

Bill could see it too, for I heard his soft whisper from a few paces back. "That's the girl. Just drop your fly as if it were a real bug. Make it skitter." Presentation of the lure was everything: alight, dart, twitch, skitter as if the hook and feathers were really some beautiful insect. And I did it. I could feel the rightness, the liveness of my lure, and that rightness gave a wild exhilaration to the deeply peaceful night.

The excitement was reinforced with every splash of feeding fish, then multiplied many times over by a splash that became a close-sequenced series of splashes that meant a strike. Bill had a fish on. The silvery glints and cascades and the sounds of his leaps were focused by the vast black quiet night. The delicate contest of Bill and the trout seemed to be over too quickly, and Bill was coming toward me to show me his prize and suggest that I change to the fly he was using.

My fish struck just as Bill reached me. The excitement I had felt in my casts, the splashing and Bill's fish, was engulfed in a wave of exhilaration. Every nerve was electrified, every cell straining to exert itself in the subtle battle. The hardest part was restraint—to maintain a touch just strong enough on the line, with no more than enough pressure to keep the rod tip up.

I moved by reflex, instinctively sensing the right response to sensations I had never before experienced. The actions themselves dictated my reactions as clearly and emphatically as those reactions had been explained to me many times before on dry runs, but now the line and the rod throbbed with the strength and wildness of a trout fighting for his life.

My left hand stripped in line, feeling the awesome strength of the trout in his runs and jumps and throbbing, vibrating battle against it. My right hand pulled now harder, now easier to exert just enough force to keep the rod tip up, yet leave the fish free to run. I had heard the words describing what I must do many times, but my real instruction came from my opponent, whose every move generated a counter move that was based on some unlearned, basic instinct. That instinct took over, superseding all awareness but that of the contest, until it was ended and the trout in a net I didn't remember reaching for, caught there on one pass through dark water which obscured the fish completely.

It was an eighteen-inch trophy brown. I was stunned. The size, the beauty and the heaviness of the fish in the net turned the excitement of my anticipation and the adrenalin-charged thrill of the struggle into mute, still awe.

I came out of my near trance of amazement when I became aware of Bill whooping and chattering beside me. I felt my blank stare turn into a smile, the smile into a wide grin, the grin to a laugh and through the laugh, I roared a shout of triumph.

I had my first lesson in taxidermy that night. My catch was too superb to just eat and remember. Bill slit the fish's belly and eviscerated it, then very carefully lifted and peeled off the skin. When the skin was free of the flanks, he sliced off the filets and I poached them while he cleaned out the head (especially the brain and fleshy cheeks) and treated the skin with borax.

The lunch of Cold Poached Trout with Dill Sauce the next day would have been enough to make me a confirmed trout fisherman for life, but when Bill wrapped the treated skin around a papier mâché armature the next week to complete my trophy, I became a fanatic.

I began to pursue my pipe cleaner scheme with a vengeance. To my surprise, Bill did not oppose it. In fact, he thought it was sensible for me to concentrate on one small area for awhile, and was delighted with the frenzy with which I pursued my new avocation.

Soon my collection had hundreds of little bits of colored chenille, and vials of dye for custom coloring at the stream to match the insect of the day. Every dawn of every weekend day we were at the stream, and my pipe cleaners were connecting regularly throughout the season. Now and again, Bill would suggest that I was ready to move on to traditional flies, but it was impossible for him to argue with the obvious success of my specialization.

I had learned the basic tools of the art and the rudiments of their use. The soft actions of the split bamboo rods and the tapered lines matched to each began to feel right as I mastered the motions of the basic casts: The overhead, rod down, pull up in a gradually accelerating motion to twelve o'clock position, pause for the line

to all but straighten out behind, flick down to ten-thirty position, ease down to nine o'clock position just as the fly drifts down. The roll cast, one smooth, fast motion from twelve o'clock to nine o'clock that picks up the line in front of it in a gigantic loop and literally rolls it forward. The steeple cast, a back cast stopped short of twelve o'clock to shoot the line straight up instead of back, to avoid tangling brush and trees. I learned to net my catch head first if possible, to prevent a last-second escape.

I started to notice that our stream was not one mass of water, but had many different characteristics in its different spots, and that those characteristics determined the presence and even the probable size of fish. The deep pool that held smaller fish during the day might have a monster after dark. Overhanging bushes or grasses were always a good spot for fish feeding on insects which had fallen from the foliage above. The eddies caused by rocks or bends in the stream were generally productive, as were spots sheltered by fallen trees or in undercut banks. The best results seemed to come from places offering the fish cold water, a nearby current (to float food past him) and some shelter or protection, as trout are inclined to be quite nervous. When we took a lunker out of a perfect hole, we would always return to the spot, as there was usually another large trout there within a day or two. It seemed that even with my maverick specialization, the traditional expedients of practice and observation resulted in better and better catches.

We feasted on trout all that summer. On weekends, we would breakfast on little nine-inch brook trout caught earlier in the morning. Cold Poached Trout with fresh Dill Sauce and Truite au Bleu were regular, and superb, lunches. And on special occasions, we would smoke our catch for one of the most elegant dinners imaginable.

Smoking trout is not as difficult as it would seem. Either fresh or frozen trout can be used. If fresh, the trout need only be eviscerated and lightly salted and peppered inside to be ready to smoke. Frozen trout (just as they come from the stream) are thawed and cleaned just before thawing is complete. Immediately after cleaning, their insides are lightly salted and peppered, then allowed to finish thawing.

Our old smoker is a remarkably simple Swedish gadget, consisting of a box, a lid, a rack and a stand. Pulverized wood goes into the bottom of the box, the rack is put into position, the fish is placed on the rack and the box is sealed with its airtight lid. Then the box is set on its stand over a kitchen range burner for twenty minutes and the fish is smoked. Only two trout can be smoked at a time, and one trout is needed for each person, so a large dinner takes some advance work. Fortunately, smoked trout keep very well, and need not even be refrigerated if prepared a day or two in advance. Just before serving, we prepare the Horseradish and Cream Sauce that makes the Smoked Trout ambrosial.

Cold Cucumber Cream precedes the Smoked Trout and Caviar Blinis follow with well chilled champagne, with red raspberries in champagne for dessert. The meal is a succession of delicate, exquisite tastes. No single taste dominates, but all build and interact, like the individual brush strokes of a pointillist painting, to create one sublime, integral sensation in this ultimate feast.

Despite the idyllic and exciting pleasures of the stream and the delicious rewards of our feasts, something was missing from my enjoyment of trout fishing. I couldn't begin to know what it was, I could think of no way to improve or increase the joys of our trout experiences. Yet I felt that there was a way.

I found that way the next year, thigh deep in a cold, wild mountain stream in spring thaw. The missing quality had been the spontaneous strength of the tumbling cascading water. The club had duplicated the fishing conditions of a natural stream, but no man-tamed brook could duplicate the thrill of battling the frothing vitality of the stream itself.

My felt-soled waders slipped over rocks shaped and polished by centuries of fast water into smooth spheres that offered no grip or footing. While wrist and mind and eye sought to battle trout, my whole body battled the buffeting water. I had planted a javelin firmly in the bottom downstream, an arm's length away, for steadying myself. A hundred feet upstream another shaft gave support to Bill.

As the stream engulfed my legs, the aura of the place engulfed my senses. Massive pines marched down the sides of the mountains that flanked the stream, their rough-barked trunks like giant pillars supporting a green-needled roof. Beneath the pines, the forest

floor was bare except for a thick carpet of brown needles, the roofs of decades past, dry, yet decaying with a rich, clean earth-smell that hovered trapped in the vault of the forest.

The pines' perfume was subtle here in the stream, its power diluted by the rushing water. The surging currents, which had been tranquil snow on a mountainside a month and several miles from here, had in their strength a strong intoxication that made me want to immerse myself completely in their frothing purity.

Upstream, the powerful beauty of the water was accentuated by the elegance of Bill's casts and the delicacy of his fly alighting on it. His control was perfect, his mastery of his art complete. Every cast was an exquisitely rehearsed ballet, every motion so known and disciplined that the sum of the motions was fluid freedom. The line floating in the water, the flow of arms and body, the flaggellum-like rod, all focused on the free flight of the celestial serpent of line with its feather-dressed, trout-deadly fang at its end.

The perfection I saw in Bill's casting, I felt in my own. It was as if each cast had a life and form that started somewhere inside me and was actually only mirrored in the action itself. The rod was at the ten o'clock position, flicked to twelve, swept down to

*It was as if
each cast had
a life and form
that started
somewhere
inside me and
was actually
only mirrored
in the substance
of the action
itself.*

*We serve
smoked trout
preceded by
cold cucumber
cream and
followed by
caviar blinis and
well chilled
champagne.*

eleven in the physical realization of a feeling of a perfect cast that was within me.

My colored chenille darted and skittered on the edge of a small whirlpool. Bill's elegant flies alighted on the water near an overhung bank. His fastidious traditionalism and my maverick's individuality flew like steel-shanked pennants at the ends of our lines. But for those tiny flags, our styles were the same, but those flags, the almost invisibly small lures, defined the entire meaning of every cast we made. The differences were complementary. I was fascinated with Bill's elaborate correctness, he was amused with my freeform *élan*. That day the fish were traditionalists.

When we stopped fishing at noon, Bill had three glistening, eleven-inch brookies. I had none. Bill gutted his catch at the stream's edge, and we cooked them on a small fire on the bank. As the fish roasted on their green twig spits, we were absorbed into the green life force of the woods, and in turn, absorbed the vitality that was engulfing us. The mystical sense of union we felt with the majesty of the forest, the strength of the stream, now musical and beautiful beside us, and with each other in shared exhilaration of absorbing and being absorbed, totally regenerated, resensitized our psychic beings; as the trout, now turning golden brown would refresh and reward our appetites and palates.

We have tasted brook-fresh trout and the revitalizing thrill of their capture many times since then, and in many places. In the spring, summer and early fall we are on streams and lakes savoring the new and renewed pleasures of the contest and the catch. Bill's proper flies or my radical chenille always seem to produce enough fish for superb city feasting the year round, but the best trout feast of all is always the one we enjoy at the stream, the reward of the abundant catch.

Feasting on Trout

Smoked Trout

4 brook or rainbow trout
Salt
Freshly ground black pepper

Slit and clean medium-size trout. Do not remove head or tail.

Salt and pepper inside.

Prepare smoker by sprinkling powdered wood on bottom of metal smokebox.

Insert rack, place trout on rack.

Slide vacuum-sealed lid closed; place smoker on medium heat of kitchen range for 20 minutes.

Remove from range and lift smoked trout off rack with long wooden spatula to avoid breaking skin or fins.

Repeat procedure for additional trout, allowing 20 minutes' smoking time for each.

Serve with Horseradish and Cream Sauce garnished with garlands of watercress.

Horseradish and Cream Sauce

1 cup applesauce
½ cup heavy cream
½ cup horseradish
Salt
Freshly ground pepper

100

Combine ingredients; blend well and chill.

Caviar Blinis

8 ounces Iranian caviar
1 pint sour cream
2 cups pancake mixture

Prepare your favorite pancake mix, making it of a slightly thinner consistency than ordinarily called for.

Drop a tablespoon on a moderate grill and allow to brown on one side before turning.

Allow 6 silver-dollar-size blinis for each person. Keep blinis warm in folded napkin on heated plate.

Combine caviar and sour cream, blending carefully with wooden spoon to distribute grains evenly.

Arrange 3 blinis on each plate; scoop on a generous serving of caviar mixture. Place 3 more blinis on top, and garnish with final small scoop of caviar cream.

Serve with chilled champagne.

Cold Poached Trout

1 large trout (16 to 18 inches)
2 tablespoons chopped shallots

3 ribs celery, chopped
6 peppercorns
3 cloves
1 cup white wine
2 cups cold water
2 sprigs parsley
2 sprigs chervil
2 sprigs thyme
2 bay leaves

Combine all ingredients, except the fish, in bottom of poacher.

Bring to a boil and simmer for 10 minutes.

Allow to cool in poacher.

Clean trout; do not remove head or tail.

Butter poacher rack and place trout on it; lower into poacher.

Slowly bring to simmer; cover.

Continue simmering very gently, for 20 minutes.

Remove trout and cool.

Serve with Dill Sauce.

Dill Sauce

1 cup mayonnaise
3 tablespoons water
1 teaspoon lemon juice
1 tablespoon finely chopped onion greens
1 tablespoon finely chopped chives
3 tablespoons chopped parsley
3 tablespoons chopped fresh dill
3 tablespoons catsup

Place mayonnaise in mixing bowl; add water and lemon juice and
whisk until creamy.

Blend in remaining ingredients.

Chill.

Truite au Bleu

4 live trout
8 tablespoons vinegar
4 quarts boiling water

Trout must be kept alive until seconds before cooking.

Kill fish with sharp blow on head; slit and clean instantly without
disturbing the film that covers scales. Hands and trout must be
wet during rapid cleaning. Do not wash fish. Plunge quickly into
boiling water and vinegar; lower heat and simmer gently for 10
minutes.

Remove fish from liquid carefully; drain well.

Serve on napkin with melted butter and new potatoes.

Garnish with parsley.

Trout Meunière

4 trout
½ cup milk
2 tablespoons flour
4 tablespoons oil
6 tablespoons butter
Boiling water
1 tablespoon chopped parsley
Lemon juice

Season trout, dip in milk, then flour.

Sauté in hot oil until golden brown. Remove to heated serving dish.

Discard oil from skillet.

Add 6 tablespoons butter and cook until it foams, turning golden brown.

102

Put chopped parsley in a sieve and pour boiling water over it; drain well.

Sprinkle parsley and a few drops of lemon juice over trout, then pour on frothy butter.

Trout-by-the-Stream

4 brook or rainbow trout
Salt and pepper
Watercress

Construct 4 spits of sturdy, forked twigs; sharpen prongs.

Make fire of available dry branches and arrange spits in front of it.

Slit and clean trout; sprinkle with salt and pepper.

Open trout out flat; skewer onto sharpened prongs through gills.

Cook for 12 minutes or until golden brown and tender.

Serve with garlands of fresh watercress which can generally be found in the vicinity of a freshwater stream.

Chapter 9.
Bass by Night

Striped bass are best pursued at the change of the tide on a calm midsummer night. It is not the best season for the fish—on eastern Long Island that comes in early fall—but the best time for the fishing experience. The beaches are nearly empty then. The surfers have gone home by fishing time, and most other fishermen won't come for one more month. Perhaps three lights will show along the mile-long beach, two head-strap flashlights and a fire—three other men pursue the first fish of the fall run, but, more important, enjoy the solitary pleasure of that pursuit.

We come at 2 A.M., two hours before the tide will change. The water's high now, the beach a long silvery peninsula paralleling the shore, defined by the vast black water behind the white foam and the sickle of black that slips between it and the highlands save at this one sand bridge that we're crossing.

It's a half-mile trek from the car to the spot we fish, and every yard seems longer through the soft sand, every step harder when we're encumbered in our chest-high waders. We carry rods and sand spikes, tackle box and blanket, and a mass of miscellaneous equipment dangles from web belts at our waists. We pass one fisherman, moving well behind the backswing of his cast as he hurls his lure beyond the offshore bar. No word is exchanged, and none will be exchanged when we pass the next man, two hundred yards farther down. Surfcasting is a private sport, and we do not intrude on the solitary efforts of the men who share it with us. If one has caught a fish he will pause in his casting to hold it up, and we will detour to him and talk a minute of lures and tides. At the end of the night's fishing, "No fish. How did you do?" and "None. They're not here tonight," will be repeated for perhaps the hundredth time by us and the man who fishes down at the point. We know each other, even though our dialogue is varied only by the vagaries of luck. He is the man who fishes the point. We are the people who fish at the rock. We share a common quest, but more, we share the contentment of the pursuit of it. Our unit is a couple, his, himself. To each it is the basic unit of existence, the solitary unit with which the solitary trophy striper is hunted. Even at the height of the school-bass season, when the regulars are augmented by a picket fence of anglers' rods, privacy and right of place are respected. There is no crowding, no conversation. Just a line of individuals, with perhaps one other couple, spaced twenty yards apart over a mile of shore, as if each twenty yards were an isolated universe.

But now the isolation is real. The headlamps of the men we passed on our way down the beach are too far away to be seen. The fire a quarter mile farther on is bright, but with a light that moves and changes of itself, independent of the man who lit it. Our only company is a boulder in the sand, a singular, massive interruption of the smooth regularity of the beach.

Bill begins his casting while I collect some driftwood for a fire. I meander down the shoreline alone in a small circle of visibility, moving in an empty world of elements reduced to their simplest forms. The water stretches in a smooth mass to my left, the land is a solid line of cliffs to my right, the sky pure space above. The white foam is the only moving thing, and its whispering slap the only sound in the still, flat-textured night.

I find any driftwood within two hundred yards, and turn back toward our rock. Now the foam is not alone in its movement. Bill's light arcs back and forth across it as he swings out his casts to the offshore bar. When the fire is built I join Bill in the evening's work.

My rod is twice my height, the lure a quarter pound of tin. Only with perfect form can my strength make them work. I wade into the surf to gain ten extra yards and start to throw. Right foot planted firmly back, left forward, carrying no weight. Right hand up by the reel, line on the pad of my index finger, left hand down at the butt. The rod is poised aimed at the horizon, then whips up, then out, in two fast moves. First back and up, beyond the vertical, to whip the rod back. Then, just as it starts to spring forward, pivot and shift onto the left foot, pull down with the left hand, push forward with the right, and let the line slip off in the middle of the downsweep. Then wait long seconds until it seems that the lure should be almost all the way out and flick the reel crank to engage the bale, stopping it taut to prevent a backlash.

At first there is no way to tell how straight or far the cast has gone. The dark obscures the lure in flight, the slap of surf masks the landing splash. The answer comes when reeling in. Does the line go straight out? How long must I crank? These are the only clues. I wind long and the line runs straight. Good. Now repeat the pattern. And again. And again throughout the night.

I pivot, pull, push, absorbed in the power and rhythm of the casts. By four I am exhausted. Shoulders and arms ache from the strain of aiming every cast at the turbulent water I cannot see, behind the bar submerged in the dark.

My rod goes to the sand spike, and I go to the fire. It is low, a warm orange flicker. I throw on some wood I had reserved and submerge in the warmth and light of its burning. Now I watch.

First Bill's casts. His power and years of experience are probably worth twenty-five extra yards of accurate casting, as he goes through his clockwork moves. Wind up, spring forward, then stand, stand and reel as the lure comes in, then wind up again. After a few minutes of watching the long-beat metronome of Bill's casts I lie down in front of the fire and let myself be drawn into the depths of its fascination.

Time has changed. We could be a millennium ahead or behind the present time. The fire and pursuit of bass are age-old. This beach might have held a fishing couple when it was first formed and, although it has probably gone through cataclysmic change since then, it seems that this could be a night soon after its formation. The boulder is the newest thing, an incongruous token left by the last glacier on its retreat north, waiting to be reclaimed by the next glacier, whose coming seems not all that remote on this night of strangely structured time.

Beyond the circle of firelight the night is all in shades of black. The cliffs behind are pure, flat black. Bill and the boulder are silhouetted black against the almost luminous blackness of the water reflecting the heavy dusting of stars whose radiance accentuates the vast darkness of space.

The warmth of the fire is like a caressing massage after the work of casting and the chill from the damp night. I squirm until the sand is shaped to me, then doze.

I come out of my sleep slowly, aware of another presence, and see a dog lying near me, waiting for me to wake. He gets up and comes to me, then lies down again, snuggling close for warmth and company on this night so infinitely black and vast that even he felt the isolation and the eerie sense of suspension in timeless time that I had felt before I slept. And so we stay, while our two companions fish—his a quarter mile away, mine but fifty feet, yet both beyond our universe of beach-fire sun and sleeping planets.

We wake with the first grey light. The fire has gone out but still I see my friend. The light has wakened him, too, and dispelled the empty night that brought him to the fire. As he slowly walks away he fades to an indistinct moving shape, then to nothing, as if he were an apparition come to comfort me, and having done so was dissolving back into the now dissolving night.

The light comes softly. I notice a pebble, visible ten feet away. Now a washed-up tree trunk thirty feet down the beach becomes an outline against the sand. I can see Bill more clearly now, still hurling a still invisible lure to fish still miles and months away. The grey is slightly lighter in the east, though the first faint pink has not yet come. Then I see the bottom lines of clouds, their tops still lost in lightless grey. The coming sun first sketches out their shapes, then adds the slightest hint of color. That color brightens, then gains the strength to reflect that brightness to the beach, giving it a light base coat of pink.

The first sandpipers appear, darting on wet sand like windup toys, skittering off as foam rolls up and threatens to dampen their delicate feet. Bill's casts are now for the flight of the lure and the perfection of the throw, and not for the hope of a fish. When the first red slash of light streaks in from the horizon his line comes in and we start home. No fish. No strikes. Not even a nibble. And we expected none. The striped bass is a rare boon granted by the surf as a reward for homage paid over months of fishing nights. The striper fisherman must be content to take the beauty of those nights as his catch, and accept the rare catch itself as a prize bestowed for excellence in a contest whose forms and rites he knows, but whose rules are unfathomable.

Patience alone is not enough to catch the striper. Although almost all casts are made into water in which no bass are feeding, they must be made properly, to the right place, with the correct lure and equipment.

The proper cast is a long one. Every extra foot of water the lure moves through on the retrieve is an extra chance for a hungry bass to see it. The lure should fly straight out both to gain the maximum distance from shore and to avoid tangling the line of a neighboring fisherman during the peak season when the beach is crowded. The tool for the job is a surf rod. The rod is usually eleven feet long, and should be one piece for the best whip action. The guides must be of graduated sizes from about two and a half inches nearest the butt to a quarter inch at the tip. This tapering effect gives minimum interference to the line as it coils off a spinning reel or moves from side to side of a conventional reel spool.

We occasionally augment our rods with kites, if we think the bass are feeding beyond casting range. The rod is put in a sand spike and the line attached to the bottom of the kite with a clothespin.

A stiff offshore breeze can take the kites out two hundred yards, and the buffeting of their lines is like a substitute tugging for the fish that so seldom come. Their vivid color against the bright sky offers a startling contrast to the black on black of the beach at night.

We steer and pull, centering each kite over the spot we think might hold a bass; then we tie the kite string down and jerk the rod to release the fishing line for the long retrieve.

The only drawbacks to kites are the reliance on the wind and the necessity to make two retrieves (lures, then kite) for each chance at a fish.

The reel is a heavy-duty model with space for enough line so that a hundred-yard run after a long cast doesn't strip it bare. We prefer spinning reels, but the conventional reel seems to present a greater challenge filled with thirty-six-pound-test braided Dacron line.

We cast our block tin lures in three basic patterns. One, fairly flat, is for surface-feeding bass on calm nights. There is a heavier, thicker model for fishing below surface foam and spindrift and a long thin lure of triangular cross section for bottom fishing. All are designed for realistic motion rather than realistic appearance, since it is the flash, not the shape, of bait fish which attracts stripers.

We occasionally take along a few spare rods and cast out live eels, hooked through the back. The rods are left in sand spikes while the eels swim around on the bottom. The eels are generally not as effective as a tin lure with a strip of pork rind on the hook, but bass action is so rare that we don't want to pass up any opportunity, no matter how slight.

In picking a spot at the beach, current is the main consideration. Strongly moving water and the rough water over bars and bottom obstructions are best. School bass like to feed in surf, while the big loners prefer the strong undertow. These preferences aren't invariable, however, and an occasional cast into still water can't hurt. My first few months of striper fishing had me convinced that all the equipment and lures and time spent in the pursuit were part of a game expert fishermen played when their skills made catching other fish too easy—a game of pursuing a mythical fish. For in those first few months I caught no fish and saw none caught in all the long fishing nights of our quest.

The first strike was more a shock than a thrill. I was retrieving absent-mindedly, expecting nothing, when a jolt bent the rod almost to the water. I yanked up against the force of the fish as he stripped line off the reel; then I held and cranked. The line kept going out as if I were doing nothing. I braced the rod against my hip and pulled up with all the strength I could find, but it wasn't enough. The reel's drag was set firm, but even the slightest pause in my straining cost ten yards of line. The fight between the fish and me had divided itself into two battles: the fish against the lure with which he was being pulled in, I against the reel from which the line pulled out. The line itself was tactical terrain we each struggled to gain. I controlled that on the reel, he commanded that in the water. A vibrating no-man's land was taut between the rod tip and the waves. If I was winning it was wet from its recent submersion, and droplets flew off at every tug and counter tug. As I lost ground the line would go out dry.

The throbbing might against which I cranked soon left me with a throbbing weakness in my arms. I could not force my hand to turn the reel against the strength of the runs. I managed to wrestle back some line each time the bass paused to gather strength, but he controlled the contest, and picked the times of his runs and rests.

At last I froze, and could not move my arm at all. One hard sprint had taken forty yards, and I could not crank them back. If the line went slack the bass would throw the hook, so I backed away from the surf to keep the pressure on while I tried to will my muscles to keep at their work.

The fish sensed a weakness as I found my strength, and he conquered another twenty yards of monofilament. But he had started to weaken, too. I got back thirty yards for the twenty he had taken, and turned him in toward shore. Now I prevailed. I determined when he could run, when he must come in. Still it was slow, and my arms tried to cramp a dozen times, but there, too, I had my way, and willed them to keep up their work.

I saw my opponent as he jumped on the start of a final run. He was only about thirty feet out—much closer than I had thought. The sight of him, and the realization of how big he really was, seemed to add to the pull of the line on his last run for his life. But it also reinforced my determination to land him, and I held him back.

Though the bass was beaten he did not surrender. I had used up the last of my energy when I saw him in the backwash. It was over. I relaxed for one split second and was jarred by Bill's shout, "No! No! Keep the rod tip up! Keep reeling!" The fish had twitched toward the sea in response to my mistake, but his strength had been spent, too, and I recovered in time to hold him in the foam while Bill ran up to gaff him.

The months of casting and long minutes of cranking had made striped bass seem invincible, and my triumph was as much bewildering as it was thrilling. It didn't seem possible that I had caught the trophy being held up to me.

Bill's delight was not diluted by any puzzlement. It was pure elation. Our path back to the car passed close enough to the stands of the regulars for them to see the fish and ask what bait and place had been the right combination. Bill's pride in deferring the answering to me (for the questions were always directed to him) was more than it would have been if he himself had caught a bass three times the size of mine.

The conversations were a bit longer than usual, since Bill couldn't resist volunteering that it was my first bass and that I had caught it with no help from him. The men who had fished the beaches for years deferred to me as an honorary expert with their questions on where I had cast, and why, and what sort of retrieve I had used. As they admired my tactics, they admired my catch. My awe was beyond admiration. Even as I heard myself describe my plan and methods (as if it had been anything but pure luck on an idle cast), I couldn't believe that I had actually hooked and landed the monster stretched on the sand for our admiration. He was one solid muscle in a suit of overlapping armor plates, silvery-glossed even over the bold black stripes that ran down his flanks. The bass seemed at least three feet long, and had to weigh fifteen or twenty pounds. He didn't have a streamlined fish shape, but a strong, chunky form that recalled the strength of his fight with me. By the time we reached the car, dawn was near. The struggle of the catch at the end of the long night of casting had exhausted me, and I curled up to nap on the drive home. I woke with bright sunlight in my eyes, and not at home. We were parked in the little village near our country place, Bill asleep behind the wheel. The day was well started—we must have been there for hours. I shook Bill to see if something was wrong—five more minutes would have had us home.

Through a yawn he explained that the ritual was not yet over. I must now have my fish weighed and measured for the local contest. That news was as refreshing as a full night's sleep, and I literally pranced into the tackle store to have the honor done.

The proprietor was more pleased than even I had been. For months we had come to him for line and swivels and feathers and hooks for our lures. For months his paraphernalia had served in a losing

We occasionally augment our rods with kites, if we think the bass are feeding beyond casting range.

cause. Now his line had hauled in this striper, a swivel of his between line and hook, the barb of a hook he sold the fatal weapon. His delight redoubled when a few regulars drifted in to witness the weighing-in ceremony for "our" fish. The scale and yardstick shrunk the monster of the beach to twelve pounds and two and a half feet, the best, so far, in the women's division.

I was happy to be heading home to bed, but the festivities were just beginning. Bill devised a special champagne sauce for my prize, and a way to eat it and have the trophy, too. He slit the fish's belly from below the gills to the anus and cleaned it out, then peeled back the skin from the flesh on the sides. Next he cut the flesh up from the bones, and we had two pure white eighteen-inch-long fillets. While one fillet poached, he dressed out the rest of the skin and dusted it heavily with borax. The unused fillet was frozen. When the champagne sauce was ready, Bill woke me from the nap that had begun as soon as I got home, and we shared a feast of my victory and initiation in the contest and mystery of the catch of the striped bass.

Feasting on Striped Bass

Striped Bass in Champagne Sauce

4 fillets of striped bass
4 tablespoons butter
1 tablespoon minced shallots
12 medium fresh mushrooms, sliced
1 cup fish stock
2 glasses champagne
1 cup white cream sauce
3 tablesopoons heavy cream (hot)
Salt
White pepper

Melt 1 tablespoon butter in large shallow pan.

Sauté finely minced shallots until transparent.

Add mushrooms and cook until tender.

Add fish stock and 1 large glass champagne and simmer gently for 2 or 3 minutes.

Arrange bass fillets in liquid; season and simmer very gently for 10 minutes or until tender.

Remove fillets to a heated serving dish and keep warm.

Reduce sauce by ⅓. Add white cream sauce, 3 tablespoons butter, hot heavy cream and one small glass of champagne.

Allow to simmer 2 minutes, stirring constantly.

Pour over striped bass fillets; serve at once.

Fish Stock

Head, tail bones and scraps of striped bass
1 quart cold water
1 quart dry white wine
1 tablespoon salt
2 onions, sliced
2 carrots, sliced
10 crushed peppercorns
4 cloves
6 sprigs parsley
2 sprigs thyme
2 ribs celery (with greens)
2 large bay leaves

Combine all ingredients and simmer for ½ hour.

Excess can be refrigerated in a glass jar for up to 10 days or frozen for longer periods.

Mediterranean Bass

12 fresh mushrooms
6 tablespoons butter
3 tablespoons chopped shallots
1 cup fish stock
1½ cups dry white wine
3 tablespoons chopped parsley
2 tablespoons basil
1 teaspoon oregano
4 fillets of striped bass, medium sized
12 mussels
12 steamer clams
12 cherrystone clams
1 young boiled octopus
2 tablespoons flour
Salt
Freshly ground black pepper

Gently sauté mushrooms in 2 tablespoons butter in shallow pan. Add 1½ tablespoons chopped shallots; sauté until transparent. Add fish stock, ¾ cup wine, 2 tablespoons chopped parsley, basil and oregano. Simmer for 5 minutes.

Arrange bass fillets, which have been seasoned with salt and freshly ground black pepper, in liquid; poach slowly for 15 minutes. While striped bass fillets are poaching, sauté 1½ tablespoons chopped shallots in 2 tablespoons butter in heavy kettle.

Add ¾ cup wine and 1 tablespoon chopped parsley and simmer gently for 5 minutes.

Add scraped, bearded mussels and scrubbed hard and soft clams. Steam for approximately 10 minutes. Shake tightly covered kettle throughout steaming.

When shells are opened, remove mussels and clams from kettle. Pour liquor carefully into heated bowl, avoiding sandy sediment on bottom of kettle.

Clean kettle and pour liquor back into it.

Lift bass fillets out of their liquor with long spatula; arrange on heated platter with octopus, mussels, hard and soft clams and mushrooms. Keep warm.

Combine bass liquor with mussel-clam liquor and cook down to ½ original volume.

Knead together 2 tablespoons butter and 2 tablespoons flour, add to liquor to thicken. Pour liquor over fish.

Sprinkle with chopped parsley.

Serve with crusty Italian wholewheat bread and chilled white wine.

113

Boiling an Octopus

1 young octopus	5 peppercorns
Boiling water	4 sprigs parsley
Cold water	3 slices lemon
½ cup olive oil	4 sprigs thyme
2 tablespoons lemon juice	Salt

Remove the mouth, anus and eyes, using scissors.

Turn inside out; discard pouch and membranes. Do not puncture ink sac.

Trim off and discard the tips of tentacles.

Wash well in running water. Dry. Pound vigorously on wooden block with large wooden mallet.

Place in cold water, bring to boil, simmer for 2 minutes, drain, plunge in cold water and remove at once.

Marinate in olive oil and lemon juice for 1 hour.

Combine peppercorns, parsley, lemon slices and thyme in a kettle of salted boiling water.

Drop in octopus and boil rapidly for 10 minutes, then simmer for 1 hour.

Keep octopus warm; arrange on serving platter with striped bass, mussels and clams.

Chapter 10.

Le Sport Bleu

No other pursuit in our year-round schedule of hunts and harvests begins like the catch of the bluefish. Instead of a quiet stalk on a snow-covered mountain or a lazy wait for nibbles on a lake, *le sport bleu* starts with pandemonium—a prolonged dash through New York's evening rush hour traffic to the *Glory,* sailing out of Sheepshead Bay. The boat and the bay are a solid hour's aggravation away from our apartment, but despite that handicap, the very special pleasures of bluefishing have made it one of our favorite sports. And it's one that we can enjoy any night we like, even when we're in the city.

The irritation of the traffic evaporates as soon as we get to the pier. The party boat area of Sheepshead Bay is like a fishing village, surrounded by the city, but not touched by it. Two hundred yards north of the water a stream of commuters' cars inch by on an elevated expressway. To the west, Brooklyn's high-rise beachfront apartments file past Coney Island to blend with Manhattan's skyline. Overhead, with metronome-like regularity big jets roar into their final approach to Kennedy Airport.

The steady murmur of the cars on the expressway and the recurring crescendo of the jets form a background against which it is actually possible to hear the small sounds and silences of the bay: the greetings of the crew and the regular fishermen, the loading of the boxes of baitfish, the quiet conversation we share with the captain on the dock. Words touch on the intricacies of the fish and the weather of last night and last week, but their meaning is: "Welcome. Be comfortable here."

Half an hour before the seven o'clock sailing time the captain begins his final preparations for the night's trip and we take a walk by the water. The road on the bay is dedicated to fishing. The south is lined with piers and boats, the north with the tools and fruits of their work. Tackle stores, fish markets, seafood restaurants and fishermen's bars, all share with us a common purpose, the only topic. The barman brings us the news of the morning's catch with our brandies, the new filleting knife we buy comes with speculation on the fish it will later be used on.

At five of seven it's time to get aboard. The *Glory* shares the single-mindedness of the bay side. Bollards and pipes and shielded lights all look functional, with no unnecessary prettification or disguise. Brass is either palest yellow or palest green, well cleaned

or awaiting greater need to clean. There is rust where rust doesn't matter, and clean paint where it might. Everything about her is solid good work, well made, well kept and well used. Even the foot-high red letters that spell out her name on the front and sides of the pilot house serve a function—from a hundred yards away you know you've been successful in navigating through Brooklyn and have come to the right place, and fishermen on other boats know for next time which boat got out first, and caught her fill, and got back fastest.

The sign "Bluefish—7:00 P.M." squeaks down and a long grating whine starts the thump and click of the diesel. Horns blast and ricochet up and down the line of boats and we back into the channel. By five past seven the whole fleet has cast off and is moving out to the fishing grounds.

We file through the inlet, past the tall buildings of the beach, the tall buildings of New York beyond them. As the boat rounds the point of the inlet, the Verrazano Bridge and the Coney Island parachute ride add their exquisite and incongruous silhouettes to the panorama.

The diesel thumps come faster now and to them and the clicking of valves two new sounds are added: the hiss of the bow wave and the mechanical rumbling of the chum grinder. The mates work at making bait, their flashing knives carving silvery strips from the backs of the baitfish, the deck lights, now brighter than the failing daylight, intensifying the metallic shining, while the silvery-bloody heads and tails and bellies of the fish are ground to a madder-rose pulp.

The west sides of the waves of the wake are rose pink, shimmering in the last light of the sun. Their iridescence is matched by streaks of glittering pink slashing across the southern faces of the east-west swells, flecked with black shadows and set off by the deep receding black of their easterly sides. This is the beautiful time. The mates finish their work on the bait and come to the western rail. Every night for half of each year they see this sight and every night it compels this quiet half-hour of appreciation in the two-hour run to the fish.

The light of the sun and the water gives way to the lights of the boat and the quiet time gives way to quiet talk. The mates speak of their appreciation of their lives and of the regulars who come to share this central part. Their hope is that you too will share, if only for a night, their realization of the abundance of experience there to appreciate. They are past masters at absorbing and being absorbed by the beauty of time, more concerned now with drawing you into the essence of the thing than going farther themselves. They have arranged and ordered their lives to give them full measure of this rare feeling and, like apostles filled to satiation with their joy, find greater joy in sharing what they have. The talk is of many things: the other fishermen—which is the artist, which the manufacturer—but mostly which the best fisherman; the vagaries of water and sky and fish; and the essence of it all, the enjoyment of the experience. All are articulate and perceptive about the beautiful, simple world they've made for themselves, with the special intelligence and awareness it took to decide just what their lives were to be about. When you go up to the bow to taste the spray, they understand that, though the spray is cold and wet on a cool damp night, the feeling of it is necessary to the feeling of the night—and they go and feel it, too. The conversation drifts into the galley to take in the boys doing evening apprentice work in the arts of living, while we take in their food and coffee. We eat the beans and franks. We drink the beer and soup and coffee, all good, all cheap, all hearty, to sustain us in our pursuit of sumptuous feasting. Below, four regulars pursue mild luck in a low-stakes card game. We are all enveloped in the close warm cabin, the players contained in the close warm hull below, an open passage making talkers and players one within the throbbing of the boat. The boat, the talk, the game roll on. Outside a man sleeps in the warm stream of air that drifts through the grating over the engine. Below two sleepers flank the poker players.

The pulse of the diesel stops and, stopping, halts all the lesser rhythms of the boat. Cards and talk and coffee are left and fishermen and mates and cooks go to their rods. The rods were tied to the rail when we set off, the four-foot intervals reserving their owners' space. The hissing of the bow wave stops and the captain comes on the loudspeaker with "Let's try it here, please."

Small buckets of bait stand on the deck beside each rod, with pails of chum beside those of the mates. The mates flip ladles full of

chum out on the water, to sink and spread and call in fish. Then the bait goes on. There are buckets filled with chunks of menhaden—two-inch squares from the silvery backs carved off the fish ground for chum—and four-inch smelts. Two types of bait are offered to accommodate two conflicting theories, one or the other of which is adhered to religiously by all real bluefishermen. The first holds that it is impossible to catch bluefish with any sort of bait except that used in the chum. The other holds that it is impossible to catch bluefish with the same sort of bait used in the chum. Practice would seem to indicate that when the blues are striking they will take any bait presented to them, whether it's been used in the chum, completely different from the chum or somewhere in between, and proponents of both theories tend to bring in very similar hauls. We feel, however, that this is the result of some extraordinary chains of coincidences, and that anyone who wants to catch a blue had better use a bait that isn't one of the chum ingredients.

Picking past the menhaden chunks (which do seem to be working for the man down the rail, in complete defiance of all sensible laws of nature) we pluck out smelts for our hooks. The point of the hook goes in one eye and out the other, then the smelt is pushed down the hook's shaft and hooked through the top of the back about an inch behind the eyes. An ounce sinker goes on the line about two feet up from the bait, and it's time to fish.

Until someone has caught a fish, the right depth for the bait is a matter of luck and guesswork. Instead of just letting the line drop down, everyone pulls it off the reel by hand, counting the strokes. Then, when the first fisherman connects, he calls out the depth and we all adjust our lines to his. With bluefish it is especially important to have lines out at different depths as the schools tend to vary over only about a five- or ten-foot vertical span of water. Occasionally, a few larger fish will loiter ten or twenty feet below the school depth, but trying for them is an uncertain bet in a sport whose main attraction is fast, frequent, almost guaranteed action.

The best depths to try vary with the season. When they make their first appearance (from early spring in the South to late spring in New England) the blues run deep. They come closer to the surface as the season progresses, except during exceptionally hot weather, when they go down again. By the time the best fishing comes, at the very end of the season, they may be up to within ten or twenty feet of the surface, and occasionally schools actually feed right up on top. The best starting depth is worked out by checking with the fishermen who were out in the morning or on the night before, then determining if the fish in the area are likely to be larger or smaller than theirs (depending on the migrations of the schools). If the fish should be larger, the line must go deeper; if smaller, closer up. Then the variables of water temperature, the location of the baitfish and the darkness must be considered. The mates know the best probable depth and are happy to pass it along.

The baits go down and the wait begins. The only sounds now are the putting of the generator and the occasional splash of the chum on the water. The fishermen line the rail and watch the waves, even though tonight the fish are probably twenty feet down. Everyone aboard but the captain is tending the row of rods that jut out over the water at regular four-foot intervals from bow to stern.

Some rod tips twitch to give the bait some movement. Some are as still as the rocking boat permits. Again, we follow two firmly held opposing theories with no demonstrable difference in results. Bill and I keep our rods perfectly still, knowing it's the only way, knowing the rod twitcher to our right will get his comeuppance (and not a fish) tonight for frightening the blues with his spastic jerks.

The sky is black now, and the sea is blacker. The boat is a cone of light and substance suspended in a void. We're twenty miles from land—within forty miles of twenty million people—yet it seems that all tangible reality ends where the light ends, twenty feet out. The whole population of the universe is this two dozen fishermen. The universe's only occupation is their patient, quiet waiting.

Then the universe gains another galaxy, glimmering four miles away. It comes closer and another shines where it had been. They both move closer still, to accommodate a third light out on the limits of perception. They move in a random pattern, then stop to drift, three bright cones like the bright cone we are. Waiting for fish, as we are.

A ladle of chum splashes into the water every few minutes, each mate tossing it out at random, as his mood and fish sense dictate. Up in the pilot house the captain talks to the three boats and to others that are out of sight, as easily as we might talk to our neighbors at the rail.

We stand for an hour, two dozen people, each within four feet of the next, each in his own silent communion with line and rod and water, while the captain maintains constant communication. Finally, someone finds the fish, not here on our rail, but a half hour's run away. The boats all share the fish when they're found. The schools are enormous, especially those of medium-sized fish, and by trading finds, everyone on every boat is virtually guaranteed a good catch. The loudspeaker comes on with "Lines up, please. We're going to move to another spot." The baits are in and the rods tied to their places for the trip. The mates make the round of the bait buckets, topping them up with fresh bait, though little bait was used. Once again we notice the cold. By the time the bow is throwing off hissing foam, three men are asleep on the hatches. The rest move into the galley for more coffee and more talk. Someone goes up to the bridge to find out where we're going.

The next spot is in the acid waters near the harbor. Some boats there have hit a big school of ten-pounders and they think the fish will stay. When we get there everyone is at the rail before the engine stops. The fish have been biting throughout our half hour run. Maybe they're about to finish feeding. Maybe they'll go down. Maybe they'll move off. When the engine is stopped, rods are untied and hooks baited before the *Glory*'s forward momentum is spent. We stop at one end of a line of boats that float like islands on water that is a sulphurous, ominous green beneath the deck lights. We can see the bent rods and wildly moving men hauling in flashes of silvery blue-black on the other boats. Then the chum splashes out and our lines go down. Menhaden and smelts carry the honor of their opposing theories to the arena twenty feet below, where the others are getting action.

Every fisherman aboard is supercharged with adrenalin as we drift down over the fish. The entire line of boats drifts over the school, while they're striking. When the boat at the head of the line drifts past the school, it starts up and goes back to the end of the line for another drift. Now we're at the end of the line waiting to get over the fish.

Suddenly a shout from the stern signals the start. "I've got one on!" and it begins. Every fisherman concentrates on willing a fish onto his line and watching the taut arched rod of the man who connected first.

The first blue is horsed over the rail—it's about ten pounds. Everyone appraised it, weighed it and tasted its baked fillets in the millisecond that it flashed in the air above the rail. By the time it is thrashing on the deck, all attention on the boat is focused on the tips of the rods. Then the blitz starts.

As I hear three men shout in unison my rod takes a sharp jerk toward the water, and before I can think I give it as sharp a jerk back up to set the hook. My hands vibrate as the rod throbs with a powerful being's defense of life. The tip points down, the handle points down, and between them the shaft bends up like a quivering rainbow. I hold and crank against the always surprising strength of a fish fighting a battle in his element.

Eventually the mechanical advantage of the pole and the uneven contest of strong line and sharp steel bring him up. Now I see him, strangely slow, in the water beneath me. He moves left, then right, and I lower the rod tip to the water as he turns again. As he starts his deliberate zigzag back to the left, I jerk the rod tip up and over the side. He thrashes through the air, and hits the deck hard. A mate runs over to unhook him, and he goes into the burlap sack that completes the catch.

I spin toward Bill to shout my triumph, but there is no time for him to hear it. Just as I turn he flips a fish out of the water and onto the deck between us. I bait up and lower again. Again a strike. Again the throb of the fight, and the arc of rod becomes an arc of silvery blue fish flying over the rail. A mate is there unhooking—the mates have all stopped their own fishing now to unhook the fish that cascade over the rail and cover the deck with their thrashing. Only the more experienced fishermen unhook their own blues. The bluefish's mouth is a long mass of small, conical teeth from front to back and side to side across the palate and tongue. One hard grinding bite could mutilate or sever a finger. The mates work fast and gingerly, wrenching the deep-set hooks from the tough cartilage of jaw. The blood starts now, in vivid-red watery streaks from the wounded jaws. It blotches the deck and stripes the glossy flanks with an extra gloss of gore.

If the fish were bigger the mates would be almost overwhelmed with frenzied action. These fish are just small enough to horse over the rail with rods. Five pounds more and a gaff would be needed. Even now an occasional big fish brings calls for the gaff and a mate runs with a skewer to help with another contender for the biggest-fish pool. Still there is frenzy. The blues hit hard and often. The school moves through the water like an animated, multi-toothed scythe, decimating everything in its path. Blues bite and rend off one mortal morsel from the baitfish they encounter, and streak on, swallowing as they go, to bite again. Another blue may devour another part of the bitten fish, but enough debris floats to the surface to ensure a flock of sea birds over any day-feeding school.

This wild, vicious appetite of the blues is their weakness—they slash through the sinking bits of chum and bait and attack with the same maniacal viciousness they would vent on a real school of baitfish. The hooks and lines are not noticed in the bait, the bulk of the boat above does not deter their blood lust. And so they are hooked and caught. Our arms ache from pumping the rods, our wrists ache from cranking the reel, our burlap sack bulges with heavy fish.

The bluefish thrashes through the air, and hits the deck hard. A mate runs over to unhook him, and he goes into the burlap sack.

*The fish are
delicious, and
the pleasure of
eating their
firm, juicy yet
flaky flesh is
multiplied many
times by the
tiredness and
excitement we
still feel from
their catch.*

Our lines go down again to twenty feet. They stop and we wait, arms tense, wrists tense, ready to set the hook. Our fingers are wrapped tight on the rod. but attuned to the slightest pull that is the beginning of a strike. But no pull comes. One man in the bow has a fish on, but the fishermen the rest of the length of the boat wait, as we do, for a strike they know will not come. The school has gone. We fish ten minutes more. Our sack is bulging, but it could hold more and our table could hold more for the feast tomorrow night—really tonight, as the late night has turned to early morning.

The armada breaks up and scatters as each boat hunts for a last spot for action. It's one o'clock when we get to a place the *Glory*'s captain thinks might hold a few more hungry fish and we try again. There is no time for a run to another spot. Each boat is on its own now, and all boats have gone to their captain's one special spot for late-striking blues.

Our lines go out to different depths again—there are no other boats getting fish here to use as guides. The chum goes out. We wait again, not as solitary as before, not as intense. Success and fatigue have relaxed us all, but still we all watch the water.

Ghostly white shapes flit through the chum slick in jerking spurts. A tired fisherman starts to reel up to snag a surface-feeding blue, but they are only squid. We wait, sleepy now in the cradle rock of the boat, and watch the water.

Then the man in the stern, the first to connect during the blitz, connects again. He calls out, "Fish on. Twenty-five feet." And once again our lines follow his to the lucky depth. We wait, the action slower now. A fish is on in the bow, then I feel the jolt that means a big one. Out of the sleepy calmness of the wait comes the wild excitement that sustained us in the first action. I pump and crank and ache against the fish, in heavier, harder fighting than with the earlier catch. I call for a gaff and a mate runs up. The long pole flashes in the water, then flashes splashing blood and fish and water over the rail. This is a big one—twelve pounds at least. Maybe good for the pool money.

The action is slower here. One or two at a time the men fight their fish, but most rods are waiting for their bites. I reel in for the night and sit on the cabin over the engine watching Bill waiting for his big fish. He hooks it and I am amazed. Did I dance and squirm like that? Did my arms and face and body strain so? The thrashing here on deck must be the mirror of the thrashing of the fish—a fatal converse of his every move. The gaff goes down and up and a gorgeous fish pounds the deck right at my feet. Bill rushes to subdue him, and our fishing's done when the blue is in the sack.

Some others fish ten minutes more and then it's two and time to turn toward home. As the boat swings north, the weighing-in begins. A mate has set up a balance in the stern. On one side hangs the biggest fish of the first angler there. The other is an empty hook on which we each hang our heaviest in the hope that it will pull the balance down. I try and lose, Bill tries and loses, but then someone else succeeds, and the first fish is taken off and replaced by the new king of the cast-iron scale for others to try to unseat. Finally the last fish has been tested and the undisputable heavyweight of the night is found. His captor collects the pool—we had all put in a dollar when we left the dock, each expecting all the

dollars for himself—and the cleaning starts. Some men scale and gut their catch, some fillet and skin. We have a simpler way that takes full advantage of the way we cook later. The wooden planks hinged to the rail go up, and one at a time the fish come out. Bill lays the fish out on their sides and cuts across the body from top to bottom, just behind the first lower fin. Then he slips the knife in and cuts along the skeleton toward the tail, lifting the freed flesh as he goes. The fish are then flipped and the other side stripped of its flesh. The pieces are then wrapped before they're put into the sack, to keep the scales of one piece off the flesh of another. The rail is lined with fishermen working at the cleaning boards. Clean cuts turn the taut hard fish into flaccid skeletons festooned with heads and tails as the flanks are cut away. The planks are scarlet with blood in the bright deck lights as the brilliant knives cut into shining fish.

The cleaning done we settle back for the run back to Sheepshead Bay. The poker game starts up again, the bunks and hatches are full of sleepers. And we stand on deck savoring the feeling of fatigue so deep that our senses have no strength to resist the sensations of the night, and savoring the saturation of sensation this surrender of senses brings.

By five in the morning we're home asleep. At eight that night the feast begins. The fish are baked under a thick blanket of parsley and butter in a pan lined with aluminum foil. The skin side of each fillet goes down on the foil, so the skin stays stuck behind when the flesh is lifted off.

While the fish is baking, we broil some thick tomato and zucchini slices to add some color to the serving platter and some strong contrast with the subtle-flavored blue. The taste of a bluefish just hours out of water is a very different sensation from the taste of a fish-market blue. The really fresh fish is very subtle and not at all pungent. The fish are delicious, and the pleasure of eating their firm, juicy yet flaky fillets is multiplied many times by the tiredness and excitement we still feel from their catch, twenty miles and twenty hours from the city terrace where we savor them and the tales of their capture.

Feasting on Bluefish

Baked Bluefish in Butter and Parsley

Serves 12

4 extra large bluefish fillets (2 eight-pound blues)
Salt
Freshly ground pepper
½ pound butter
1 bunch parsley, finely chopped

Preheat oven to 425 degrees.

Line large, shallow baking pan with aluminum foil. Place fillets close together, skin side down on foil. Sprinkle on a generous amount of coarse salt and grind fresh black pepper uniformly over the fillets. Dab large chunks of butter closely over entire surface and cover with a thick blanket of finely chopped parsley. Bake undisturbed for 30 minutes, then begin to baste every 5 minutes for an additional 15 minutes.

Chapter 11.

Fishing the Lakes

Lake fishing is a lazy day of muted colors and mild excitements.
It starts in the soft grey of first light, on the soft grassy side of
a small country lake. Our old cedar canoe slides down the dew-wet
bank and splits the glossy smooth surface of the water with tiny
ripples so explicit as they cut the surface stillness that their gentle
disruption can be traced a dozen yards away.

I clamber to the bow. Bill takes the stern and pushes off the last
half yard from shore, and we move away from the lakeside canopy
of low limbed trees into a doubled world. Matching halves of a
symmetrical universe meet and are suspended on the reflecting
plane of the surface. Ahead, the farther shore rises and hangs from
the central line, flanked above and below by the now pink glowing
sky, the soft rich depth of green receding in the roseate brightness.
We, too, are split, suspended, in the split universe, but our converse part ripples in the rippling wake of the canoe. We do not
see ourselves but rather see the wood with which we work. Rod,
paddle and boat—bamboo, ash and satiny glowing cedar—smoothed
by a half century's use, all shimmer in the wavelets' serried rise
and fall.

The only sound is of the occasional quiet paddle strokes that slip
us through the water, and even that is absorbed and dissipated in
the fast dissolving mist. We glide toward lily pads that float out

127

from the farther bank, their outer fringe perhaps a hundred feet from shore. I cast as Bill paddles us across. There will be no fish here, but the long languid arc of the fly rod is a graceful partner to the short languid stroke of the paddle, curving pirouette embellishments to the geometrically straight course of the canoe. It does not matter that these casts will catch no fish. It will not matter much that later casts will. Our goal is pan fish: perch, pike, pickerel, bluegills and crappies. But the only purpose of the goal is to give a semblance of structure to this beautiful moment of unstructured time.

This early in the day and year the fish we seek will be beneath those pads or at their edge, about two yards below. The lake is spring fed and the water is clear, but still I use a bright-yellow streamer for easy visibility in the shade of the surface plants.

No fish come yet, but soon they will. We slip along the rim of the plant raft, making exploratory casts into the open spots and along the edges. We're fishing, but not really. The essence of the day is the enchantment of the peaceful time, shared by Bill and me, and by the dear old friends, the boat, the rods, the streamers, that accompany us in this sweet and private moment.

And then we are not alone, as one of my retrieves is interrupted by a slight tugging at my line. Little vibrations come up the light fly line and shake the rod tip. A tiny tremor vibrates down the bamboo shaft. I stop my retrieve until a few more minuscule taps at the line say that the bait has been taken and that the fish is on. A flick of the rod tip sets the hook, and I reel in the fish. Not much more effort need be spent than is used in bringing in the empty lure. I straighten up the rod and give an extra crank to bring the bluegill into the canoe.

The fish goes into the sack down in the bilge, and the yellow streamer flies back to the spot. Bill casts now, and each fourth cast brings in another half-pound fish. Half an hour's casting later more than a dozen little bluegills fill our sack. Perhaps that many more were hooked and got off. Some get away when we try to set our hooks too soon, before their little nibbling strikes have let them really take the bait. Others escape when their weak-willed fight finds help from weak-walled mouths and the hooks pull free. Two dozen fruitless casts mean that the school has moved, or has finally been frightened from their feeding by the mild thrashing of their hooked companions. Bill stops his casts and paddles once again as we seek out the next fishing spot.

We next find crappies, close cousins to the bluegills, their fight and size and look almost the same. They are feeding slower, or they are a thinner school, for an entire hour drifts by as we pull out an even dozen fish. By then it's almost noon. The fish have stopped their feeding, so we will stop for lunch.

We glide to shore and I collect the wood for a fire while Bill cleans the catch at the lakeside. Scaling and gutting the little fish takes time and I begin to fry the first few that he finishes while he cleans the rest of the bag.

I build a small fire flanked by rocks and set a cast iron skillet over it. A bit of butter goes into the pan and is well melted when I've chopped off the fish's heads and tails. The meal is ready when Bill's cleaning is done—fried fish and cold white wine. We spread out on the bank and relax in the shade. The fish is crisp and sweet, set off by cooling wine. The shade here on the bank is cool and has the sweet smell of the leaves and grass, to reinforce the sweetness of the fish. Our lunch gives satisfaction to appetites piqued by the morning's freshness and the morning-fresh fish, and amplifies our appetites for the afternoon's efforts.

No fish will bite now, so we let the wine and languor win and nap a bit on the soft grass of the lakeside. Two hours pass in light and lovely sleep, and then we glide back onto the stillness of the lake. An hour more goes by before the fish return, this time feeding on insects on the mirror surface.

Off to the right we see the tiny circular ripples that mean a surface-feeding school, and I change from streamer to dry fly. Bill paddles us upwind of them, and we let the breeze drift us down. The circles multiply to overlapping rings, and start to move away downwind as our canoe is blown noiselessly but slowly along. I try a roll cast to the school, but my fly drops two long yards short of the goal. Bill takes one quiet stroke, the fish stay up, and this cast finds the fish. I retrieve for fifteen feet, then cast again, and now a firm yet dainty tug taps at the line. The line vibrates, with the fear and not the strength of the quarry, and I jerk the rod tip up to set the hook. Each third or fourth new cast brings in a fish for our fish fry to come. Bill is catching too, with a bravado display of control. He puts his flies into the lily pads, then tugs them into the water, as if they were bugs falling from the plants. It gets him no more fish, but adds an element of finesse to the simple harvest of these easy-biting fish. The perch don't stop biting, but soon we catch our fill, and change our flies to streamers to try for white bass inshore.

Bill paddles down the shoreline, perhaps fifteen yards off, as I cast at the mossy base of the banks. I cast ahead, so the quiet sounds of our paddling will not send down the school, though if they dive, their haunts are so shallow that the tempting lures can draw them up.

We move past banks as though we're slipping past exotic shores of unexplored streams. The canoe moves quietly, with stalking stealth, while at the bow the probing line rolls out and rolls out again to find the home of the swimming treasures. At last it comes. The tap again. A thrash of line, a well set hook and a white bass joins the perch in the bilge.

We stop and cast again, but this one bass is all that we can get. One more slow, quiet round of stroking paddle and swinging rod on the placid stillness of the lake and we go in.

Our sack now holds more than three dozen fish, mixed nicely for a fine fish fry. We might have done with a few more bass, but even without them the catch has been good. Ashore we clean the perch and solitary bass and add them to the morning's assortment as we add the memory of the day to those of many other days spent in pursuit of the fish first pursued by almost all men who fish. The recollection of a bluegill or crappie caught on a first fishing trip, or even one caught a fishing lifetime later, is still most people's outstanding fishing memory despite many stronger strikes and bigger fish since then.

That well remembered early trip, at least for me, was not much like this latest lake fish day. Bill's object then was sure success despite my lack of skill. I could barely hold a fly rod then, and certainly could not cast it well. Our gear was a more basic panfish rig.

I started on a light glass rod and spinning reel designed to work in the least nimble hands. Our bait was not a streamer or a dry fly, but just a worm threaded on a simple hook. A sinker carried

*The world is
doubled now,
matching halves
of a symmetrical
universe met
and suspended
on the reflecting
plane of surface.*

Mixed nicely for a fine fish fry. The catch has been good.

it down to the fish and a bobbing float told me when to set the hook. That trip too began in early morning in the early spring. But then the object was not just to spend a pleasant day, with fish an incidental bonus, but rather to achieve sure success to cement my budding fishing interest.

It worked, and probably always will. A worm sunk down two yards in clear cool lake water will probably always induce some pan fish to have a taste. A bobbin disappearing beneath the surface will always tell the brand-new angler when to set the hook. No line or rod or reel that I have ever seen will fail to bring in at least half of the fish so hooked, and no one I have ever known has not been hooked himself by the elation of that first success.

Of course, in time, most fishermen will add details to make the catch more fun. Fly rods to demand the skill of casting. Dry flies or streamers to eliminate the sure appeal of a natural bait. But still and always the appeal of a day spent after pan fish is and will be the pleasure of the day itself and the assurance of a successful catch.

Feasting on Pan Fish

Baked Marinated Pickerel

6 pickerel (marinated)
6 tablespoons butter
1 tablespoon finely chopped lemon rind
1 tablespoon finely chopped parsley
1 tablespoon finely chopped basil
1 tablespoon finely chopped chives
Salt
White pepper

Remove fish from marinade; season with salt and pepper; arrange in buttered baking dish.

Cream butter with lemon rind and herbs.

Dot herb-butter generously on top of each pickerel.

Bake in a 350-degree oven for 20 minutes.

Turn fish; return to oven for 15 minutes, basting frequently.

Serve with lemon wedges.

Marinade

1 cup dry white wine
2 tablespoons vinegar

2 tablespoons olive oil
1 lemon, thinly sliced
1 carrot, thinly sliced
4 cloves
1 bay leaf
2 sprigs parsley
2 sprigs thyme
8 peppercorns, crushed
Salt

Combine ingredients in earthenware dish.

Arrange fish in the liquid so that it is completely immersed.

Marinate for 2 hours.

Braised Carp

2 tablespoons diced onions
1 carrot, diced
3 tablespoons chopped mushrooms
2 sprigs parsley
1 bay leaf
½ teaspoon dried sweet basil
1 4-pound carp
1½ cups fish stock
½ cup white wine
2 tablespoons butter
2 tablespoons flour

Arrange vegetables and herbs in baking dish; lay clean scaled fish on top; season.

Add fish stock and wine.

Cover baking dish and bake in 350-degree oven for 1 hour.

Remove fish and skin it; arrange on heated serving dish.

Keep warm.

Cook liquid down until it is reduced by one half.

Knead flour and butter together and add to sauce to thicken.

Strain sauce over fish.

Pike in Sweet Cream

6 small pike
1 tablespoon lemon juice
6 tablespoons flour
6 tablespoons butter
3 tablespoons heated brandy
1 cup heavy cream
Salt
Freshly ground black pepper

Clean pike.

Rub the insides with lemon juice; season with salt and pepper;

roll in flour and brown well on all sides in foaming butter.
Pour heated brandy over fish and ignite.
Add salt and pepper to taste.
Add heavy cream and bring to a boil.
Arrange fish on heated platter and strain sauce over it.

Pan Fried Perch, Bluegill or Crappie

6 fish
2 lemon slices
2 tablespoons flour
½ teaspoon sweet basil
¼ cup butter
Salt
Pepper
Parsley sprigs

Rub the insides of the cleaned fish with lemon slices.
Roll fish in flour seasoned with salt, pepper and basil.
Sauté in foaming butter over high heat until golden brown on
all sides.
Serve on heated platter; garnish with sprigs of fresh parsley.

133

Chapter 12.
Frutti di Mare

A quarter mile down the beach a couple shimmer in the water. They move in to the shore, then out, then in, always exactly ten feet apart. Their deliberate patterns, now parallel, now spiraling, form and dissolve so slowly that they are barely discernible when filtered through the rippling heat waves of the fire hidden in the pit in front of me.

Straight out, halfway to the horizon, a small boat darts and bobs across the water, marking each stop with a bright flag planted in the waves, a troupe of varicolored flags dancing behind it.

Up the beach, where it juts out in a bar, three groups repeat three different sets of movements, like sets of parts on an intricate mechanical toy. One group, just at the waterline, stoop, reach, stand, filling glistening sacks at their sides. Past the bar kneel diggers, clawing up piles of wet black sand, moving, and clawing again. Farthest out, in the water beyond the bar, two couples rake the bay, like careful gardeners tending liquid grass.

The couple down the beach suddenly break the languid patterns of their dream ballet and move faster and together onto the beach. They squat on the sand and transfer handfuls of flashing silver from the net on the beach to the ice chests beside them. The white-bait, incomparable hors d'oeuvre of the *frutti di mare,* has been harvested.

All of the movement around us has been carefully choreographed to produce the ingredients of the supreme feast of the fruits of the sea at the pinnacle of their flavor. The silversides in the ice chests will make a mound of crisp-fried whitebait that would be enough for a week of tantalizingly small and wildly expensive appetizers at any gourmet restaurant, all to be devoured as mere prelude to the meal. Mussels, gathered by simply bending to pluck them up, fill string bags for a first course, while the harder-won main courses are pursued by the crew of the lobster skiff and the diggers and rakers who search for the hard- and soft-shelled clams. The fire is burning well, the tables are set up on the sand, the sea lettuce has been gathered and the wine is chilling. Our work is done for now, and Bill and I can relax and watch the harvest.

For years we had tried to gather the ingredients of the *frutti di mare* ourselves, but producing them all at the right time and with the perfect freshness that makes the meal sublime was more than the two of us could manage. We either had to buy some of the ingredients, and so, for us, turn our gala feast into an excellent meal but no cause for celebration, or work continuously for two days before the event and have little energy or spirit for celebration, even with cause aplenty. We decided to try sharing the experience of the catch as well as that of the feast with our friends. We weren't sure that they would be able to find the delicate skills and subtle pleasures of harvesting the sea, but we devised a simplified plan to help them master and appreciate their tasks.

The adventure begins at our country house at eight on an early summer morning. Each couple is assigned to the capture and preparation of one course of the meal and given a sheet of step-by-step instructions. We keep the fire building and housekeeping chores for ourselves so we'll be handy in case anyone needs help or advice. A fast breakfast and we're off in a caravan to the beach. Each season we look over several favorite spots for *frutti di mare* on our early spring fishing trips and select one that promises the richest harvest.

The abundance of ingredients varies tremendously from year to year. Mussel beds, which seem as indestructible as the beach itself, can be washed away by winter storms and shifting shorelines.

Silversides can suddenly appear where we haven't seen them in years of fishing. Clams can disappear for no apparent cause, or flourish a year after the first seedlings appear.

We arrive at the beach a little before nine—the day was picked because low tide is three hours before lunchtime and all of the catch but the lobster is best gathered at low tide. Everyone sets off after his quarry; Bill and I set up camp.

The first job is making the fire. We dig a pit about two feet long, a foot wide and a foot deep into the sand. It is filled with charcoal or driftwood, and the fire is lit immediately. Next we gather the fresh sea lettuce that gives the subtle beach flavor to our meal. After we have about a half bushel, we set up some portable tables, put the wine on ice, and await the return of the mussel gatherers. Collecting mussels is the easiest part of the catch of the *frutti di mare*. Mussels grow in incredible profusion in beds that often stretch, blue-black and glistening, a hundred yards along the low tide line. Since they live clustered on rocks—and even pebbles— above the sand, they can be had simply for the effort of plucking them up. The only difficulty is resisting the urge to scoop up every mussel on the beach.

Selectivity in gathering mussels is of three ascending orders. Depending on the skill and finesse of the gatherers, mussels are chosen on the criteria of edibility, convenience of preparation or aesthetics.

The first standard, edibility, is simple. Only those mussels which are never completely exposed above the waterline can be taken. They need not be completely submerged, but they must be splashed by an occasional wave even at low ebb tide. Each mussel's shell must be firmly locked closed, and every one must be tested by trying to push the shell open. Occasionally a shell does yield, and, if it does, it is filled with fine black sand instead of mussel. Just one of those counterfeits in the bushel would mean no clamdigger cocktails before lunch.

The usual course leading to the second degree of mussel gathering is scraping mussels gathered with only first degree expertise. We try to save our guests from the hard lesson of scrubbing and scraping their way through a bushelful of barnacles and sea lettuce, by warning and imploring them (since the housekeeping brigade shares in the mussel-cleaning chores) to pick only the cleanest and least encrusted mussels, and to knock off as many small encumbrances as possible before adding mussels to the gathering bags. The final, aesthetic, degree of mussel gathering is one which cannot be forced, and isn't even really necessary. It is, however, satisfying as only the art of making art of simple tasks can be. When Bill and I pick mussels we pick only those of the richest, glossiest blue black, of exactly identical medium size. Although it would seem that mussels all of a given size would ensure uniform cooking, there is absolutely no discernible improvement in flavor, texture or aroma of the finished Moules Ravigote. There is an exquisitely subtle visual gratification in a perfectly matched serving of Moules, but only the most ardent aficionado would appreciate it. Our selectivity is solely for the sake of the thrill of pursuit and the pleasure of meeting higher and more difficult standards where unlimited resources might make the catch simple collection.

When two clam basketsful have been gathered (the mussel gatherers fill string sacks tied to their belts—eight sacks to a bushel) they are taken out to thigh-deep water and rinsed, then brought ashore to be cleaned.

Although Bill and I have been able to heighten the challenge of gathering mussels, we haven't been successful in our attempts to lessen the drudgery of cleaning them. Every barnacle and bit of seaweed must be taken off every mussel in our bushel. Knives are the traditional tools, but we've found that long-handled wire brushes cut about a third off the time required and eliminate the wounds that knife-scraping used to inflict. We pitch in and scrape. Barnacles calcified onto the shells and sticky, clinging sea lettuce are worn down and off by the steady chafe of the wire. First the larger bits are broken off, then the final clinging bits are powdered by the monotonous rhythm of the brush. Shells, rough with encrustations, turn smooth, and hands once smooth turn rough, as the wire bristles scrape and rescrape. Sea lettuce slime yields to smooth, clean shells as the scraping goes on and on. The backs of our hands are flicked by the wires, our palms are hard from the hard wooden handles. By the time the wire clam baskets are filled with scraped mussels, someone has invariably suggested that we check Abercrombie's just once more to be sure no one has come

up with a mechanical mussel scraper since our last desperate call.
After another rinse the mussels are steamed in the biggest available clam steamer (we set it on to simmer with parsley, shallots,
sea lettuce and white wine, halfway through the cleaning). Two
ropes lead from the handles of the pot to two exhausted mussel
cleaners who shake the steamer back and forth, vigorously, while
the mussels cook.

When the shells open, the mussels are scooped out into a large tub
to cool for twenty minutes, then shucked and put into a jug of
prepared Ravigote. The jug goes into a cool (but not iced) chest
until three quarters of an hour before serving, when a mountain
of shaved ice will be packed around it to put just enough bloom of
chill on the mussels.

The mussel liquor strained from the steamer will later be the basis
of the clamdigger cocktails that mark the end of the preparations
and the beginning of the feast. After cleaning the steamer and
setting it on to boil with sea lettuce, sea water, parsley and celery
for the soft clams, Bill and I join the mussel gatherers collapsed
on the sand.

The hard-shell clamdiggers are usually the next group to return
to the feast site; they've been out in the bay scouring the sandy
bottom with long-handled clam rakes. Although it is possible to
take clams from the bottom of water two or three fathoms deep
with stilt-like clam scoops, our clamdiggers work closer to shore.
They stand in knee- to chest-high water, the rake handle over one
shoulder, and pull the shaft toward them with the prongs down
about four inches in the sand.

Every few feet, the tines come up for inspection, and another
cherrystone or two goes into the basket floating suspended in the
center of an inner tube. Once a bed of clams is found (either by
wading barefoot and burrowing with inquisitive toes, or, more
simply, by watching other clamdiggers), the clams are as good
as gathered. Like the mussel crew, the clamdiggers' real work
begins when they get back to the fireside.

After thorough rinsing in deeper water, the hard-shelled clams
must be shucked. They are opened and cut from their shells with
a stout-handled, short-bladed clam knife. The blade goes in at the

hinge of the shell and is twisted to pry the clam open. One quick circular cut under the clam body frees it, and it is ready to be seasoned and chilled.

By the time the last hard-shells are shucked, the steamer used for the mussels is boiling again in anticipation of the arrival of the soft-shelled clams, and the clamdiggers are finishing up their delicate work. The couple who amass the steamers must be extraordinarily deft and industrious. Soft-shell clams could be mashed to pulp by an amateur clam raker, so each one must be plucked from the sand by hand.

Soft-shells live between high and low tide lines. The clamdiggers set out with trowels and heavy rubber gloves, looking for the blow holes in the sand that mark the clam bed. These holes seem to be impressions made by dozens of pencils poked point down into the sand—and a few frothy bubbles at the opening are the tipoff to a clam close to the surface. When they find a good bed, the clamdiggers start to excavate.

140

They dig down at a forty-five-degree angle with their trowels until they spot the neck or squirt of the quarry, then they go after him by hand, burrowing behind until they make contact. The feeling of wet sand surrounds them—the wet grainy sand under their knees, the sucking pressure of the wet sand against their gloved hands, the chafe of the wet sand grains that fall into the gloves, the splatters of the wet sand their digging hands throw back against legs and face and body. The chase is surprisingly exciting, for the clam is a miniature jet, and can retreat quite quickly by spitting water through his nozzle neck to push himself through the sand.

Once caught, the clam can be extracted from the sand in two ways. If caught by the neck, the catcher has only to hold on until the suction built up by the clam's jet action is dissipated, then pull the little morsel out slowly and gently. If the clamdigger has overshot his mark and finds himself with a handful of clamshell, much more skill is called for. Too hard a squeeze or too fast a tug will crush the fragile shell (a broken clam is edible, but for the ultimate in steamers and hot clam broth, each clam must be intact). We tell the clammers to imagine that they are retrieving eggs from the collapsing sand. Rather than gripping at the shell, they must move their fingers forward gently until the whole clam is in their hand, then carefully cradle the clam as they pull out, shielding it from the pressure of the sand.

Soft-shelled clams require more rinsing than hard-shells or mussels. Their jet locomotion pumps sand as well as water through their necks, and if they didn't flush themselves out by pumping through clear water, the clam broth would have a rich sand base. After rinsing, the clams are covered with sea lettuce and submerged near the shoreline until after canapés and cocktails. Then they are dropped into the hissing hot steamer for approximately fifteen minutes and served first as clear, hot clam broth, then as succulent steamed clams to be dunked in crocks of melted butter and savored whole.

Since whitebait is ready to eat within minutes of coming out of the ice chests, the silverside netters keep working until the arrival of the lobster boat signals the end of the catch and the beginning of the feast. They make countless slow arching passes through the water with a thirty-foot billow of fine mesh net, straining through tons of water on each pass for nothing or dozens or hundreds of tiny fish. Their job is the most serene and yet most invigorating of all. The weight and force of the water in the net reduces all movements to their simplest and most economical forms and imposes an almost somnambulant slowness, around which flash the darting baitfish: under, in front of, around, and, after agonies of anticipation, into the net. A thousand silversides may flit into the net, then out and around it before it reaches shore. Or they may linger just long enough. But the force of millions of drops of water against thousands of strands of mesh holds back any attempt for a quick rush to the beach. The net must move in its unchangeable course at its immutable speed.

The seiners wade their way through thigh-deep water, pulling at the bamboo pole attached to one end of the net. The pole at the other end is pushed into the bottom to form the center of their radial sweeps. The net just skims the pebble bottom as they drag it in its arc. It billows across its three-foot height and all along its length to make a vast pouch. When the net is spread on the sand, the baitfish explode into silver popcorn, thrashing and hurling themselves in foot-high leaps. The netters move down the net, plucking up the edible fish and oyster crabs, and flipping the tiny ones back into water with the hope that they've learned from experience and won't show up on the next pass. The keepers (2 to 4 inches) go into ice chests so they will be chilled when they're dropped into the deep fryer.

A shout signals the climax of the catch. The lobster crew is speeding into shore. White towels wave triumphantly over white spray as the skiff skims over the tops of the swells, on full throttle. The bow takes off on every crest and slaps out plumes of foam in every trough and we race to the water in dancing anticipation.

The only time we can be sure of this jubilant finale is early in the season when hoards of lobsters migrate past the beaches in our area. Later the lobster pots would have to go out several days in advance of the feast to ensure a lobster entree even with the best of our wiles. Although we are at the time of peak migration, we still use every trick we have been able to pry out of the local old-timers to fill our pots.

The lobster talisman off southern Long Island is a white cup in every pot. It may be bait, it may dispel bad spirits, it may charm the fates. Whatever it is, it works. Our lobster trappers are always armed with one for every pot.

The lobster pots themselves are one part of the catch we haven't been able to streamline or simplify—and would never want to. Each pot is a beautiful and individual combination of intricate construction and stark functionalism. Our six pots were their maker's entire output of one long day. They are shaped like miniature quonset huts of rough-ripped oak slats, each slat an inch and a half wide and an inch and a half from its neighbor. The ends are funnels of net, although slats are often used here, too. The two-by-four foot parlours will accommodate a dozen lobsters, and if we're lucky they will be filled nearly to capacity. Two ten-pound slabs of concrete on the floor of the parlour sink the trap to the bottom.

Lobsters like cold, deep water, but only expert local knowledge can help find the right cold, deep water. In our area, the main route of the lobster migration is along the ninety-foot shelf, about two miles out. The lobster crew speeds out as soon as we get to the beach, for even at the very best season and with the most invitingly baited traps, the three hours we allow is very scant time to fill our lobster quota. The traps are baited with several fish and

*The seiners
wade their
way through
thigh-deep
water,
pulling at the
bamboo pole
attached
to each end of
the net.*

The site of the feast would seem to be the setting of a surrealist film.

the traditional white cup and lowered down to do their work. A buoy and flag are attached to the end of each line, and the bobbing flags form a hopeful and far-flung pattern as the traps are spread wide over the lobster area to give the best chance for a successful catch. After setting the traps, the lobster crew can do nothing but come to shore and wait and *will* the lobster into the parlours. After three hours of determined concentration (with occasional interruptions for swimming or basking with other crews whose preparations have been completed), they go back out to collect the fruits of their skill and willpower. Six buoys picked up and a sixth of a mile of rope hauled in, and the harvest is done. When the last pot is aboard, a sprint to a hero's welcome on the beach is all that remains before the feast. Once ashore, the lobsters are transferred to clam baskets and submerged at the water's edge until it is time for them to become the exquisite climax to the feast.

At the site of the feast, red-checked tablecloths deck two eighteen-foot, twenty-four-legged tables laden with mounds and mountains of clams and mussels and whitebait and lobster and piles of paraphernalia on the otherwise empty sand. The pale yellow curve of the crescent beach and the pale yellow ellipses of the eroded grass-topped dunes behind and the bright-noon shine of the curve of water coming in to meet the curve of the beach form endless arcing patterns washed out by the high bright light and focused on the saturation of colors of the feast site. Vivid green sea lettuce, the red of the red-checked tablecloths, deep blue-black mussels, and deep red-orange lobster—all contrapunctuated by the washed-out brilliance of the pale white wine, the pale grey clams, the still flashing though long chilled silversides, and the central focus within the focal center of the flat-glistening steamer, sun-licked and flame-licked and hissing out the steam that is the center of all.

The beach has been transformed into an immense banquet hall contained within the curving line of dunes and vaulted and expanded by the infinite metallic blues of sky and sea. Twenty-four canvas chairs become places set for Titans whose common cause is too great to be contained in any space less vast than this. The other table is laden with the splendid trappings of the feast; the wax of the paper plates and bowls of butter, parsely, spinach, onions and shallots and the glossy paper cylinders of salt and pepper catch and scatter sunlight like glistening many-faceted crystal. The chestsful of shaved ice on the hot wide beach seem only possible through supernatural will. The entire visual aspect of the feast site is one of a weirdly unreal beauty that is in absolute contrast to the voluptuous superabundance of the feast itself.

The feast begins with heat-quenching draughts of sea-scented clamdigger cocktails and meal-sized portions of cold bracing Moules Ravigote and crisp hot Whitebait Hors d'Oeuvre. The subtle flavors of the herb-saturated mussels and piles of golden, deep-fried silversides are dashed by the hot blunt taste of tabasco-laced clams on the halfshell. Next, the cold white wine that is the harmonizing thread of the meal is served with the hot clam broth that clears and tantalizes palates for the delights that follow: Steamed Softshell Clams, succulent and sweet, rich and dripping from crocks of melted butter; the firm, white sweetness of the whole boiled Lobsters; and the crispness of a cold Spinach Salad.

Chilled Fresh Raspberries in Chilled White Wine are followed by mugs of Pot-Boiled Coffee. We have all devoured more in this one sublime meal than we could normally eat in a week, but the expenditures of effort and energy required to provide the substance of the feast providentially provide the gargantuan appetites that guarantee full appreciation of its glories.

Feasting on Frutti di Mare

Feast for 24

Clamdigger Cocktails

3 quarts chilled mussel liquor (reserved from steamed mussels)
1 quart Russian vodka
Cracked ice
Dash of lemon

Combine mussel liquor and vodka in 1½ gallon jar, cap jar tightly and shake. Pour into short, round tumblers full of cracked ice; add dash of lemon juice.

Moules Ravigote

12 shallots, finely chopped
1 cup finely chopped parsley
8 cups dry white wine
2 handfuls sea lettuce

4 bay leaves
6 sprigs thyme
Freshly ground black pepper
1 bushel mussels, scraped and scrubbed

Combine in a steamer all ingredients but mussels, and simmer gently for ½ hour.

Add mussels, cover steamer and shake constantly until shells open (approximately 10 minutes).

Scoop mussels out of steamer; carefully pour off liquor into crock (avoiding sandy sediment on bottom). Chill and reserve.

Remove mussels from shells and allow to cool for a few minutes; add to large-mouthed earthen jug of Ravigote (prepared previous day and transported to beach in lid-capped jug).

Ravigote

½ pint wine vinegar
1 pint olive oil
2 teaspoons salt
¼ cup capers
1 cup finely chopped parsley
⅓ cup finely chopped chervil

⅓ cup chopped tarragon
¼ cup finely chopped chives
4 onions, finely chopped
4 shallots, finely chopped
2 fresh basil leaves
Freshly ground pepper

Combine ingredients and whisk together briskly. Float two large fresh basil leaves atop and allow to stand overnight in earthen jug. Cap jug for transporting to beach.

Whitebait Hors d'Oeuvre

1 peck silversides, chilled
2 quarts bacon drippings
1 quart vegetable fat
Salt
Lemon juice
Freshly ground black pepper
Lemon wedges
Watercress

Remove silversides from ice chests to layers of absorbent paper towel; pat completely dry.

Prepare large cast iron kettle half full of combination of bacon drippings and vegetable fat. Heat to 375 degrees. Drop cube of bread into fat; when cube browns within 60 seconds, you can proceed with the deep frying.

Scoop portions of silversides into finely meshed wire frying basket and submerge quickly into hot fat until a crispy golden crust signals perfection. Small portions are mandatory so as not to lower fat temperature.

Drain thoroughly and place on absorbent paper-toweled platter. Repeat the process, allowing time for fat to reheat after each batch.

Transfer whitebait to huge wooden platter.

Sprinkle with salt, freshly ground black pepper and drops of lemon juice. Garnish with lemon wedges and long curly strands of watercress.

Cherrystones on the Halfshell

½ bushel cherrystones
Salt
Freshly ground black pepper
Dash of tabasco or horseradish
Lemon juice

Thoroughly rinse, re-rinse and shuck clams. Open with a short-bladed clam knife, separate clam from shell. Chill. At moment of serving, add freshly ground black pepper, dash of tabasco or horseradish sauce.

Steamed Soft-Shell Clams

1 bushel soft-shell clams (steamers)
Sea water
10 ribs celery
2 bunches parsley
3 handfuls sea lettuce
Melted butter
Lemon wedges

Fill a large steamer with ½ inch sea water and add celery, parsley and sea lettuce. Bring to boil. Simmer for 15 minutes, then increase heat and add clams; cover tightly. Steam over moderate heat for approximately 10 minutes.

Scoop out clams. Ladle out piping hot clam broth into soup cups. Serve with dash of Worcestershire sauce preceding clam course. Serve steamers with crocks of melted butter and wedges of lemon. Refill soup cups with clam broth for dunking.

Beach Lobster

24 medium lobsters
Sea water (to cover lobsters)
5 handfuls sea lettuce
Lemon wedges
Drawn butter

Bring sea water and sea lettuce to boil in large steamer. Add lobsters and cook briskly for about 8 minutes. Reduce heat (by topping fire with fresh logs) and continue to cook for about 15 minutes. Drain.

Cut lobsters and spread open, crack claws, serve with lemon wedges and bowls of drawn butter.

Spinach Salad

5 pounds leaf spinach
5 large Italian onions
1 garlic clove
1 cup olive oil
24 fillets of anchovies
7 tablespoonfuls lemon juice
Salt
Freshly ground black pepper

In advance, thoroughly wash spinach leaves and slice onions paper thin. Place in large plastic bag in ice chest on the beach.

Rub jumbo wooden salad bowl with garlic clove. Transfer spinach leaves to bowl; add a little oil at a time while tossing leaves. Add anchovies, lemon juice, salt and freshly ground black pepper.

Fresh Raspberries in Chilled White Wine

10 pints fresh raspberries
2 cups powdered sugar
Chilled white wine

Rinse berries at home by running cold water—*very gently*—through their slatted wooden baskets. Transport to beach nested in large cardboard carton, all ten boxes in single layer.

Fill dessert bowls with berries, sprinkle lightly with powdered sugar, pour on chilled white wine.

Old Fashioned Pot-Boiled Coffee

1 pound finely ground coffee
1 egg
8 quarts boiling water
Pinch of salt

The night before the feast, mix finely ground coffee with egg in an earthen crock. Add enough water to moisten thoroughly and allow to stand for several hours, then place in fine muslin bag, tie securely with linen thread. At beach, drop into boiling water. Add tiny pinch of salt. Boil exactly 5 minutes. Let stand for 10 minutes. Serve.

Chapter 13.

Frogs' Legs
and Snapping Turtle Soup

The most unusual subjects of our hunting and feasting adventures are frogs and snapping turtles, and, appropriately enough, both were added to our list of pursuits and pleasures in an unusual way.

Instead of discovering them while we were on a stalk for other game, or hearing of them by the flickering firelight of a rustic hunting camp, our inspiration for both amphibian hunts came in the urbane surroundings of cosmopolitan restaurants.

In the case of snapping turtle soup, our feast preceded the catch. We were having lunch in one of the old Philadelphia restaurants, and I looked up from my menu to find Bill's face absolutely covered with a grin of delight. He didn't wait for me to ask the reason, but managed to say "They've got snapping turtle soup" without even breaking his smile. I had had green turtle soup, of course, and like it, but didn't see how the presence on the menu of snapping turtle soup merited quite so much attention.

But despite my less than unbounded enthusiasm, this was something that I obviously had to try. My grin soon matched Bill's as I bolted down the treat. It was not the green turtle soup I knew, but a thick, sherry-laced chowder with morsels of surprisingly delicate veal-like meat.

I was about to ask how Bill had known about this delicious spe-

149

cialty, but once again he anticipated my question.

"One summer a long time ago I read some James Fenimore Cooper, and it excited me into exploring every lake and stretch of woods I could find. We were staying about a hundred miles north of here, near the headwaters of the northern branch of the Delaware River, and it wasn't long before I struck up a friendship with a man who lived in a little cabin by the river. He didn't seem to do anything but trap and fish and do a little out-of-season hunting, so his cabin was a natural base for my exploration.

"One day I was looking for woodchucks along the railroad track that ran behind his place and parallel to the river when I stopped to examine a small swamp that had been cut off from the marshes at the riverside by a bend in the tracks. The cinder embankment of the right of way was streaked by slides running from the tracks down to the water. Some of the slides were almost two feet wide—apparently some big thing had dragged itself up from the river, across the tracks and then used the bank as a sliding board. The mud bank across the swamp had the same curious markings, and I was beginning to tingle with the idea of discovering some exotic monster, when I noticed the cinders of the roadbed writhing in front of me as if a giant worm were slithering through the ground," Bill continued.

"Boyish curiosity immediately overcame the initial shock I felt at the thought of the monster of my imagination being right *there,* and I peered down for a closer look. Just as I did, a small pointed nose poked up through the cinders, followed by the rest of a just-hatched turtle. Soon sixteen little black fingerling turtles were crawling confusedly around the cinders over the nest that had held the eggs they had just shed.

"I got my first and only snapping turtle bite as I was pocketing the tiny critters, and it actually broke my skin and raised a welt, even though the biter was less than an hour out of his egg. By the time I had finished poking around the roadbed, I had discovered two more nests. One held what looked like two dozen deflated Ping-Pong balls, but the other had ten more baby turtles for my pockets.

"When I displayed my catch to my friend, he was amused by my amazement at nature at work, and suggested that I take on some snappers more nearly my size. Turtles were wreaking havoc on the smallmouth bass fishing and the new mallard hatch on a favorite pond, and he thought we might have a go at them.

"His homemade traps were just turkey wire cylinders with chicken wire cones pointing into them from the ends. The cones were cut off at their points so a shell a foot and a half wide could pass through. The bait was tin cans punched full of holes and loaded with rotted chicken parts dangling in the centers of the cylinders. The way scent travels through water, the smell of those gamey wings and necks must have gone almost down to the ocean. At any rate it was strong enough to put five snappers into the half dozen traps we set out at the upstream side of the pond."

When the soup and the tale were done, I was a snapping turtle enthusiast, and had said no more than "Why don't we try?" when Bill agreed that we should go after them.

Bill's old mentor's traps were easy to duplicate, and we found an old hoop net to add to the arsenal. The net was a seven-foot-long cone of heavy netting, two and a half feet wide at the open base, a foot at the point. Bill judged it to be just perfect for trapping at the rims of the creeks that fanned out around the bay. We got ten pounds of chicken backs and necks and let them go gamey for a week. Then early one morning the snares went out. A local duck farmer was delighted to have us try to get some of the turtles that feasted on his ducklings, so a trap with a retrieving chain tied to it was tossed into the rank water of his pond. He very fervently wished us luck, but didn't foresee much, for the turtles could have all they might want to eat by swimming up under a duckling, and didn't need to go to the trouble of crawling over all that chicken wire.

Another trap was thrown into the brackish water at the edge of a marsh, the net being saved for the relatively clear water of a stream, since it had to be set out by hand, from in the water.

Our anxious curiosity began with the setting of the first trap. Before we had reached the second site we were wondering whether the first might not contain a turtle already. By the time all three were out, the suspense had grown to such proportions that we had to still it by telling ourselves that the traps had all been successful, and that we were only holding off going back because that was the etiquette of the game, and not because we thought our snares needed more time to work.

Having assured ourselves of our success, we started collecting the other ingredients for the soup.

The veal bones were roasted, then combined with all the other ingredients for a half-day's simmer. With those last pre-turtle preparations completed we lost all semblance of our self-imposed assurance, and made a dash for our traps. We dashed twice more before dark, but no snappers turned up to complete our soup. By the time we started out to retrieve the traps the next morning we thought we would have to convert our turtle chowder to vegetable soup, but the first trap came up heavy. When Bill pulled the chain it didn't budge, and our wild optimism of the day before came back, now with good cause.

A hard tug freed the trap from the mud, and when we hauled it in I saw my first big snapper. He was about a foot across, and even if Bill hadn't warned me to keep clear, I wouldn't have gone near the turtle for anything.

He rode up in the trap like a defiant dinosaur, standing braced, neck extended when it came above the surface. His neck was stretched at least nine inches out of the glossy shell, and swiveling menacingly on the end of it was a head that seemed to be all beak. Then it was all bright pink as he snarled a challenge at us, the trap and the world in general. It would have been a formidable challenge to take up. His head darted from side to side with the appearance and the speed of a striking snake. His stubby legs were tipped with half-inch claws. And head and legs and tail were covered in a loose, stretching, pebbly-grained skin that looked less penetrable than the shell itself. We decided to keep this monster in the trap for his ride to the soup pot.

When we got him home Bill propped the turtle's shell next to a log, then got him to strike out across the log at a stick. Bill tried it once or twice for timing, and on the third strike brought down a hatchet on the turtle's neck. The decapitated snapper was hung on the north side of the house to drain for a day. The ghastly sight of a headless, draining turtle was enough to keep us as far south as our property went until the following day.

Bill got up first the next morning and removed the brown-black shell. A quick scalding in a kettle of boiling water turned it creamy white; then it was added to the stock we had made on the trap-setting day. After a few hours of simmering the shell was removed, and the cut-up sections of turtle meat added to the soup, which was then cooked until it was reduced by half.

Just before serving an ounce of sherry is added to each plate. Although the flavor is pungently heady, there is a delicacy, especially in the meat, that completely belies the grizzly appearance of the game itself.

Although we had had many pleasant restaurant dinners on frogs' legs, the meal we had which led to catching our own didn't include these succulent morsels on the menu. We were having dinner with friends in Indianapolis, and when the conversation turned to hunting they mentioned a favorite of theirs that we hadn't tried: farm pond frogs.

As a reward (or perhaps a retaliation) for our introducing them to the pleasures of an all-night pursuit of bluefish on their last visit to New York, our friends decided to initiate us into the night-long hunt for frogs.

The expedition was mounted as soon as we finished dinner. First stop was our friends' house to be fitted out with long-sleeved flannel shirts, khaki trousers, tennis shoes and insect repellent. We all took flashlights and gigs, trident-headed spears that would seem more at home in the hands of Mediterranean sea gods than here, in our hands, in the middle of the Midwest. Our host carried a French wire frogging basket with a trap door that could snap shut. Our friends' farm was a two-hour drive from town, so it was late enough to hunt when we got there.

There was no moon, but the air was so clear that the pale white glow of starlight and fireflies was enough to light our way. On the way to the dock we startled an old raccoon away from his dinner, and seeing his crawfish meal gave us an idea for the first course of our coming frog feast. The dock was near the cabin, at the shallow upstream part of the lake. The glossy black water widened out gradually for two hundred yards, then stopped abruptly in the crisp, straight line of a dam.

We pushed off from the dock, and the muffled splashing of the oars and the bow wave joined the quiet gurgling of the spring fed stream which fed the lake. The croaking of tree frogs and the lowing of cattle drifted out to us as we slid over the smooth water.

An east wind had pushed the duck weed to the near side of the lake, and we started downstream just beyond the green maze. Our host took the bow, to show how it was done, Bill rowed, and our hostess and I sat in the stern and played our lights over the water.

The lights flicked over a shape against the pale green weeds, and before they could flit back the spear flashed out and back into the boat. It was a fourteen-inch bull—four inches of body, two inches of feet, and two giant drumsticks in between. The frog had been killed by the gig, so all we had to do was circle his trunk with a knife, pull off the skin with pliers and drop the legs into a plastic bag which had been liberally sprinkled with coarse salt. The remains went overboard.

Our hostess hit the next. The frog hadn't been speared by any of the tines, but was stuck between two, too fat to escape. He squirmed free just as the spear came back aboard, and jumped to escape. I saw him flash and saw and felt a wet ugly giant plop into my

lap. I shrieked and tossed him half way across the lake. He was still in the air when the purpose of the trip came back to me in a shock of chagrin. My fellow hunters muffled their laughs in sleeves and hands and hats, and I could see that I had become the butt of endless future frog-gigging jokes.

I redeemed myself as best I could with a monster frog hit right between the eyes.

We really saw action when we got down to the dam. It seemed that there was just enough time to change places after each shot before the next target appeared.

The lights flashed over water, found a shape, the shape and spear collided as the lights flashed back in an unbroken fluid circle. When we had collected two dozen frogs we headed toward the marsh across the lake.

We beached the boat and went ashore. The ground was so soft it seemed that the lush grass covered empty space. We walked up a small creek that fed into the lake, and found the crawdads. Each was stationed next to a hole in the bank, and we had to grab them before they could scurry to safety. Half an hour's frantic grabbing left us with only a dozen crawdads and we decided to call it a night. We got back to Indianapolis just before dawn, tired, but determined to get everything in order for the evening's feast. The frogs'

He rode up
like a defiant
dinosaur,
standing braced,
neck extended
when it
came above
the surface.

*A quick
scalding
in a kettle of
boiling water
turned the
black shell
creamy white.*

legs were rinsed, soaked in cold water, and then covered with olive oil, basil leaves, chopped parsley and shallots. The still kicking crawdads were dropped into boiling water and dill for ten minutes, then left in the liquid to cool. We dropped into bed in happy exhaustion—and happy anticipation of the feast to come.

Feasting on Frogs and Turtles

Snapping Turtle Soup

1 12-pound snapper
Boiling water
5 pounds veal knuckles, cracked
1 cup chicken fat
3 onions, diced
4 ribs celery, diced
4 carrots, diced
1 leek (white part only)
1 bay leaf
4 cloves
2 sprigs fresh chervil
2 sprigs fresh thyme
2 tablespoons salt
Pepper
1 cup flour
4 quarts water
2 cups canned tomatoes
1 onion studded with 4 cloves
2 stalks celery
1 clove garlic, minced
2 quarts beef stock
1 cup canned whole kernel corn
¼ cup sherry
Dash of Tabasco
4 thin slices of lemon
Dry sherry

Behead snapper and hang it upside down to drain for a day.
Plunge turtle into pan of icy cold water, scrub well with brush.
Change water several times during scrubbing.
Submerge snapper in a large kettle of briskly boiling water for 10 to 15 minutes.
Drain. Remove black epidermis and the thin tortoise discs from the exterior of the shell.

Trim all meat out of shell with sharp boning knife; cut into joints. Reserve meat and shell; discard entrails.

Put cracked veal knuckles in large roasting pan; brush with chicken fat.

Add diced onions, carrots, celery, leek, bay leaf, cloves, chervil, thyme, salt and pepper.

Roast in 400-degree oven until bones are thoroughly browned.

Sprinkle with flour, mix well and roast mixture for 30 minutes longer.

Transfer mixture to large kettle, add turtle shell, 4 quarts water, 2 cups drained cooked tomatoes, onion studded with 4 cloves, 2 stalks celery and minced garlic; simmer very gently for 4 to 5 hours until liquid is reduced by half. By this time, shell should have distintegrated.

Add turtle meat joints, 2 quarts of rich beef stock and corn; continue simmering for two hours or until volume is reduced by one-third and turtle meat is tender.

Scoop out turtle meat; trim off bone and cut meat into small pieces. Reserve.

Strain soup, which should be very thick.

Add pieces of turtle meat, ¼ cup sherry, a dash of Tabasco and lemon slices. Simmer for 10 minutes.

Serve very hot; add one ounce dry sherry to each serving.

Frogs' Legs Provençal

24 medium frogs' legs
½ cup olive oil
4 large basil leaves
4 tablespoons chopped parsley
Salt
Freshly ground black pepper
6 tablespoons butter
2 teaspons lemon juice
4 cloves garlic, finely minced

Cover frogs' legs with cold water; soak for 2 hours.
Drain and dry.

Prepare marinade of olive oil, basil leaves and 2 tablespoons chopped parsley; marinate overnight. (Optional.)

Remove frogs' legs from marinade, dry thoroughly; season with salt and freshly ground black pepper.

Sauté in 2 tablespoons butter in heavy skillet. When all sides are golden brown, arrange frogs' legs on heated platter.

Sprinkle with lemon juice and chopped parsley.

Add 4 tablespoons butter and minced garlic to skillet; bring to foam.

When golden brown, pour over frogs' legs and serve at once.

Crayfish with Dill Sauce

1 dozen crayfish
4 quarts boiling water, well salted
6 sprigs fresh dill with head

Wash crayfish in running water; remove little rudder in center of tail; discard black intestine.

Drop crayfish into kettle of boiling water; cover kettle and bring back to the boil.

Cook for approximately 10 minutes.

Drain after liquid has cooled.

Chill and serve with Dill Sauce.

Chapter 14.

The Harvest
of Jellies and Liqueurs

Among the greatest of the great desserts of Europe, counted
with the superb creations of the patisserie's sophistication, the
elaborate confections of the konditorei, is one of delightful simplicity: *fraises du bois*. These tiny wild strawberries, firm-fleshed
and extravagant in flavor, are drenched in thick cream, devoured
and cherished wherever they grow. The arrival of the *fraises du
bois* is a two-month succession of festivals that follow the path of
the ripening berries from the southernmost tip of Spain north to
the Pyrenees, across into France, up the Loire valley through
Nevers to Chartres and Paris. There have been gourmets so en-
tranced by the exquisite berries that they made annual tours accompanying the growing season around the Continent.

Although there are no such pilgrimages in the United States, there
might well be one in honor of the native wild strawberries, first
cousin to the *fraises du bois*. Although they are relatively un-
known, strawberries-gone-wild abound throughout the entire
country. They are smaller and firmer than domestic berries—
juicier, sweeter, richer in color and with the same extravagance
of flavor of the European *fraises*. They are found in abandoned
fields from March to September, depending on the local climate.
Our own wild strawberry harvest condenses the celebration into
two days. We stop by the field several times during the weeks

before the berries ripen to try to gauge the exact moment of perfection. Keeping a close eye on the weather helps. Cloudiness or
cold slow the growth and especially hot or sunny days speed it.
Usually after about two weeks of watching we sense and see and
smell a change. Suddenly the berries are redder. The few we
sample seem to have developed new reservoirs of juice and flavor
overnight. And our preparations for tomorrow begin.

This year was special. We had just discovered a new berry patch
secluded off a lonely dirt road. The delicious promise of the berries
was seconded by their beautiful companions of the field—daisies,
larkspur, cornflowers and bachelor buttons. We were on our way
by eight, with piles of baskets: baskets for berries, baskets for
field flowers, baskets for bread and wine and cheese.

When we got to the field I immediately set out to pick enough
wildflowers to fill every vase in the house. Bill was more logical.
He put up his folding stool, spread a cloth and set out the Camembert and bread to warm in the sunshine and absorb the heady

fragrances of the field. By the time Bill's preparations were made
I had gathered more flowers than my arms or our house could
hold, and we both began amassing red mountains of berries.

The actual picking of wild strawberries is simple enough to permit
an awareness of and saturation in the sensations of the field.
Hands methodically pluck and pile. Every few minutes a berry is
unconsciously eaten, and all the while mind and eye and smell and
taste are free to wander in the splendors of the colors and textures
of the meadows.

Impressions cascade over themselves. The golden rippling daisies
recall a bishop's mitre of many years ago shimmering above a
crowd, bound to the present by the pink that permeates all—the
pink of the berries, the pink of the rose petals strewn before the
bishop, the pink juice-stained fingers, the pink of the flowers on
a green silk dress, the same pale green as the waving grass, which
I wore with my first silk stockings that felt like the breeze of the
field years ago and today. The fragrances of the flowers and the
berries mingle and merge with the incense of the bishop and rede-
fine themselves as sweetness in the sweet feeling of eating sunshine
that comes with the taste of sweet, warm berries. The kaleidoscope
of pink-flecked, purple-flecked, yellow blowing daisies shimmered

and resolved itself on a stark bright patch of white and red. Bill had picked a mass of berries and was asleep beside the heap, his stillness jarring in the gentle, constant swayings of the field.

Our picnic was spread and ready. The Camembert and bread were warm and soft—an exquisite melting together of mellow flavors. Our dessert was handfuls from the pile of scrumptious berries. Glasses wet and cold from the ice and full of cold white wine toasted the beautiful harvest and washed down our feast.

The next morning we woke to jelly jars, paraffin, sugar, pectin and a sterilizer ready on the kitchen counter. To keep the spirit of the harvest celebration, we make our jelly outdoors. Bill puts up a "portable jelly kitchen" which is an oak plank across a pair of saw horses, and starts a charcoal fire in his old converted forge. We then set to hulling the masses of berries.

When the berries are hulled and ready, we sterilize linen towels in a 400-degree oven for 2 minutes and cover the oak plank with them. Next the jelly jars and tops are boiled in an old clam steamer for 2 minutes, put on the plank with tongs and covered with more sterilized towels. A large tin-lined copper pot goes on the forge, a long wooden spoon is at hand and we're set for the jelly-making alfresco.

We usually end up with so much jelly that we need every container that falls to hand, but we're always sure to have some especially attractive jars or crocks for Christmas giving. We save several quarts of berries for dessert treats and to use as a vital ingredient of the Wild Rose-Petal Jelly to be made the following week. Many other harvests will follow until well into November, but none can equal the air of ceremony and celebration of the strawberries-gone-wild. We started making Wild Rose-Petal Jelly one year when birds had stripped our regular orchard of wild cherry trees bare a few weeks before the fruit ripened. We were searching for another grove, but with little success. It seemed as if the only thing growing in the woods that year was the wild roses that rambled over every fallen log and natural fence that had a bit of sun on them. The tiny flowers filled every clearing with pink. It was mid-June, and each flower's six heart-shaped petals had just opened away from its yellow center.

The exquisite blossoms were so appealing and so bountiful that we thought up a use that would justify including them in our annual harvests: Potpourri. We keep huge bowls and vases of rose-petal-based Potpourri around our apartment, and we decided to add an exotic touch to them with *wild* rose petals.

We got some baskets from the car and began filling them with velvety pink petals. Plucking the wild petals was (and always is) a beauty-filled experience. Since the roses grow in the more open part of the woods, dappled patterns of light filtering through the leaves above constantly play over the flowers, now intensifying, now subduing their delicate pinks. The surrounding foliage is a shifting spectrum of greens from pale to near black that isolates the roses from the steady dull brown of the forest floor.

A languid afternoon's work filled all of our baskets, and we returned home to dry our harvest. As we spread the petals out to dry, their smooth, soft texture seemed much too luxurious to serve as mere decoration, and we decided to try to make a jelly of them. We spread the petals out on some handy window screens, rinsed them with a garden hose, saved a few leaves for garnishes, and got the jelly-making paraphernalia. We had no recipe (and had never heard of one for rose-petal jelly), so we decided to follow the general procedure for strawberry jelly, and put in a few baskets of wild strawberries for good measure.

It seemed that the jars for this exotic brew should be more than ordinary jelly glasses, so we hunted up some antique crystal. We've made this our practice ever since, for there are few gifts you can give more sumptuous than an elegant jar of this rare treat. We've learned since that our "original" idea of making jelly from rose petals has been a tradition for centuries in Turkey, but the deflation of our creative pride hasn't detracted from the sublime pleasures of salted crackers, brie and Wild Rose-Petal Jelly.

Septembereptember finds our country cellar jelly shelves creaking with the weight of summer's harvest. The blackberry shelf is stocked, and so are the raspberry and currant and wild rose-petal and strawberry shelves. Only the shelf marked "wild cherry" is empty. Wild cherries are small burgundy-colored pellets that generally drop to the ground uneaten. Their flesh is bitter, there isn't much of it, and what there is is attached too densely to the pit to be worth eating anyway—at least in their natural state. But crocked and turned into jelly, or home-brew liquor, they're superb.

*Every few
minutes
a berry is
unconsciously
eaten, and
all the while
mind and eye
and smell
and taste
are free
to wander
in the splendors
of the
meadow.*

A large tin-lined copper pot goes on the forge, a long wooden spoon is at hand and we're set for the jelly making alfresco.

The cherries grow in closely grouped clusters on trees of every imaginable size. When the season comes it often seems that we have as many children as there are cherries and they're all in high trees and low trees bending down branches for the ground troops to harvest milking fashion the festoons of cherries on each branch. The cherries come at a perfect time for a crop which requires mass labor—camp and vacations are over and school is still two weeks away. All children (and any of their hapless friends caught loitering nearby) are dragooned and equipped with pails and tubs and buckets. The smallest and least agile are assigned to "milking" duty on the ground while the older and abler are sent aloft to sway down the bounty. It takes a lot of pulling and plucking to fill a pail with the little cherries, but the rewards are well worth the effort. After rinsing, the cherries are divided into two equal piles to make the two indispensable accompaniments to the fall's game meals: Wild Cherry Jelly and Wild Cherry Liqueur.

The rich wild flavor of Wild Cherry Jelly is a perfect complement to a pungent game meal. In fact, it is too hearty to be eaten any other way.

The tangy fruits of the wild cherry harvest will liven dinners all fall and winter, but the main pleasure of the harvest is the lively harvest itself.

The harvest of wild growing things yields a summer of wonderfully fulfilling experiences. It seems that there is hardly a bush or tree or flower or plant around us that does not offer some exotic gastronomic delight. And it yields superb and exotic delicacies all through the year.

Feasting on Wild Fruits and Berries

Wild Strawberry Preserves

Alfresco

4 quarts wild strawberries
6½ pounds sugar
1 bottle pectin (4 ounces)

Hull berries and combine with sugar in a very large kettle.

Place on hot charcoal grill and bring to a rolling boil, stirring gently with wooden spoon—taking care to keep berries whole.

Move to area of grill where coals are burning slower and continue to boil gently for three minutes.

Remove from fire and add pectin.

Skim off foam with large metal spoon; cool ¾ hour.

Fill sterilized glasses, jars and small earthen crocks, cover with hot paraffin.

Let stand several hours, then store in cool, dry place.

Sunshine Strawberries

6 pounds wild strawberries
6 pounds sugar

Place hulled strawberries in large kettle in layers, sprinkling sugar over each layer.

Place kettle on outdoor grill and bring slowly to boiling point. When boiling begins, skim carefully.

Boil ten minutes (from the time the fruit begins to bubble), stirring carefully with large wooden spoon to prevent crushing berries.

Pour into large shallow glass baking pans with tightly fitting glass covers and place in sunny window for three or four days—or keep out on portable jelly bar, bringing pans indoors before sundown each day. The berries will grow plump and firm, and the syrup will thicken.

Fill the sterilized jelly glasses, cover with hot paraffin. Let stand for one hour, then store in cool, dry place.

Wild Rose-Petal Jelly

4 quarts wild rose petals
3 quarts cold water
2 quarts wild strawberries
6 pounds sugar
2 cups liquid pectin
Wild rose leaves

Rinse rose petals and allow to drip dry on a common house screen. Put into very large kettle with water and bring to a boil. Do not stir. Keep at gentle boil for 20 minutes.

Dampen a jelly bag and wring well, then suspend it over earthen bowl; pour the rose-petal mixture into the well-secured bag.

Allow juice to trickle through for about 4 hours. Do not squeeze (the jelly must be *crystal clear*).

As soon as rose petals have been placed in jelly bag, put hulled berries into earthen crock and mash well with wooden muddler or wooden potato masher.

Transfer berry mash into a separate jelly bag which has been wrung out with *hot* water. Allow juice to drip through for 4 hours. Do not squeeze or press. Yield will be about 1 cup.

Combine rose-petal juice with wild strawberry juice in a very large kettle, add sugar and bring to a boil.

Stir in pectin at once and return to full, rolling boil for 1 minute, stirring constantly with wooden spoon.

Remove from heat, skim off foam with large metal spoon, pour immediately into sterilized glasses.

Add a single rose *leaf,* which has been dipped into boiling water and drip-dried, to each glass.

Cover at once with melted paraffin. Allow to cool for several hours. Store in cool, dry place.

165

Wild Cherry Jelly

8 quarts stemmed wild cherries
1 quart water
5 pounds sugar
½ teaspoonful almond extract
12 ounces pectin

Put wild cherries into very large kettle; add water.

Bring to a boil and simmer gently for about 25 minutes.

Pour into jelly bag and squeeze out juice; yield will be about 6 cups.

Measure six cups juice and combine with sugar in kettle.

Add almond extract, place over high heat and bring to a boil, stirring constantly with wooden spoon.

Add pectin at once, then return to full rolling boil for two minutes, continuing to stir constantly.

Remove from heat, skim off foam with large metal spoon and pour into sterilized jelly glasses.

Cover instantly with hot paraffin. After several hours, store in cool, dry place.

Wild Cherry Liqueur

6 quarts stemmed wild cherries
2 pounds cut loaf sugar
2 quarts bourbon
1 tablespoon allspice
1 tablespoon cinnamon
1 tablespoon clove stems
½ teaspoon almond extract

Wash wild cherries and pick off stems. Fill a large-mouthed earthen jug or crock alternately with a thick layer of cherries, a layer of loaf sugar and a few of the whole spices.
Continue until jug is almost full (use second crock if needed).
Pour in bourbon until full.
Cork. If crock is used, wrap corking material around edges of crock lid to ensure tight fit.
Let stand in absolute darkness in a closet, cellar, cabinet or other dry, cool place for at least three months (the older the better).
Decant.

Candied Violets

Small basket of violets
½ cup finely ground (not confectioner's) sugar
Pure alcohol
Violet essence
Violet-color dye
6 tablespoonfuls water
3 tablespoonfuls finely ground arabic gum
3 tablespoonfuls granulated sugar

De-stem violets and dip flower heads into cool fresh water.
Remove flowers from water and carefully drain in a large sieve, allowing to dry, in a cool place, for several hours.
Spread the fine sugar on a white sheet of paper; sprinkle it with alcohol and add violet-color dye and violet essence; knead well and let the sugar dry.
In a double boiler, melt arabic gum with an equal amount of water. Combine granulated sugar with an equal amount of water over heat. Blend arabic gum solution with sugar syrup. The resulting solution should be about 32 degrees on the scale of syrups. Keep it warm. Put a few violets at a time in a porcelain pan and pour a small amount of gum and sugar solution over them.
Carefully turn violets, to coat them evenly with solution. Then dip violets, one at a time, in the dyed powdered sugar. When you

have treated all violets, spread them on a large sieve and let them dry at room temperature. It will take two or three days.

Wild Blackberry Cordial

1 tablespoon whole allspice
1 tablespoon cloves
1 tablespoon cinnamon bark
8 quarts wild blackberries
2 quarts cold water
4 pounds sugar
2 quarts whiskey or brandy

Tie spices in a thin bag.
Pick over and wash the berries.
Place in preserving kettle, cover with the water, let boil until thoroughly soft, then strain well and measure juice.
To each quart of juice add 2 cups sugar (1 pound).
Add spice bag and boil about 20 minutes or until thick.
Let cool and measure again.
To each quart of syrup, add 1 pint of whiskey or brandy.
Bottle in earthen jugs and cork tightly. Do not open for 3 months.
Will keep for years, and improves with age.

Grapes-Gone-Wild Wine

1 peck wild purple grapes
Water
Sugar

Mash grapes well and then strain and press through a cloth.
Add barely enough water to the pressed grapes to cover them.
Strain the juice thus obtained.
Use 3 pounds of sugar to one gallon of the liquid. Let it stand in a crock or wooden tub, covered with a cloth, from 3 to 7 days. Skim off what rises every morning, without disturbing the contents.
Put the juice in a cask, leave it open for 24 hours; then bung it up and put clay over the bung to keep the air out.
Let young wine remain in the cask for 6 months, when it should be drawn off and bottled.
Wine can also be poured into jugs, allowing the corks to remain very loose; when through fermenting, bottle. After all signs of fermentation cease, put in the corks very tightly and tie or wire them in and seal. Keep in a cool place.

Dandelion Wine

1 gallon dandelion flowers
1 gallon boiling water
3 pounds sugar
3 oranges, cut in small squares
3 lemons, cut in small squares
1 ounce yeast

Pick dandelion flowers early in the morning, taking care not to have a particle of the bitter stem attached.
Pour the boiling water over the flowers and let stand 3 days.
Strain and add the rest of the ingredients and let stand in earthen crock to ferment 3 weeks.
Strain and bottle.

Wild Raspberry Vodka

3 quarts wild raspberries
1 fifth of Polish vodka

Fill gallon-size jug with culled, carefully rinsed wild raspberries.
Pour vodka over berries.
Cork jug and allow to stand in cool dark place for at least 3 months.
Decant into bottles. Cork tightly. Serve chilled.

Wild Sorrel Soup

4 cups wild sorrel leaves
4 tablespoonfuls butter
2 boiled potatoes
6 cups chicken stock
¼ teaspoonful nutmeg
Salt
Freshly ground black pepper
½ cup sour cream

Thoroughly wash sorrel leaves.
Melt butter in flameproof glass skillet and sauté leaves until well wilted.
Place in blender with boiled potatoes, and blend thoroughly.
Combine with chicken stock.
Add nutmeg, salt and freshly ground black pepper.
Blend in sour cream until smooth and creamy.
Chill and serve.

Chapter 15.

Lures, Decoys and Paraphernalia

The beginning of Bill's lure-making activities actually preceded his interest in hunting and fishing. He started at the age of ten when he realized that lead soldiers he cast could be traded for all sorts of things of value to other ten-year-olds. And so, as he tells it, a cherry-glowing cast iron pot of slippery, silvery lead was always on the stove, and cast iron ladles full of molten lead filled up the martial molds. Printer's devils from a local newspaper and print shop kept the little entrepreneur supplied with typeforms which heat and skill transformed into baseballs, decoder rings and crystal sets.

He's doing the same thing today, turning old beer coils and broken pewter pitchers into lures that bring in the things we value now—striped bass and bluefish. His lure and decoy making has grown beyond the melt-and-pour simplicity of his lead soldier days, and now includes fly tying, decoy carving, taxidermy and occasional goose-call whittling, but the focus still is the liquid lead that started it all by cooling into the shape of a miniature hussar and bringing in that first coveted penknife, so many years ago.

Actually, when we can manage it, lead is used only to harden the tin which we prefer. About five percent lead is mixed with the block tin, whose velvety, translucent luster is much more desirable than the dull grey of lead alone. But sometimes, when we've been unable to track down a bar or brewery that has gone out of business and whose beer coils are our prime source of tin, we make do with pure plumbers' lead.

The work is hot and so it's saved for cold winter weekends. So many fish are hooked and caught in our minds' eyes while we make lures that it sometimes seems that these stay-at-home times are the most exciting adventures of all. They certainly are the most spectacularly successful. And when spring brings a change from imaginary to real confrontations with the fish the lures we cast while dreaming of the fruits of their later casts make us the best equipped fishermen on the beach.

If Bill and I are both making up stocks of our favorites, we work on the kitchen stove. If he's experimenting on some new molds or amassing piles of glistening tin just for the pleasure of the work (and I have discovered him melting down year-old lures only to recast the tin in the same mold to make them "this year's models") he leaves the kitchen to me and uses a hot plate in the basement.

Two burners are required—one, as hot as it can be, to melt the tin, the other, not so hot, to heat the mold so the molten tin doesn't cool prematurely and solidify before the flow reaches the bottom of the form. When that happens half-lures and lures with bubbles and pockets result.

A cast iron kettle is used to hold the tin, and a ladle is needed to put it in the mold. We prefer an old Civil War bullet ladle, designed especially for scooping up and pouring molten metal, but any sort of scoop will do. Our favorite can hold only three ounces, so large lures are poured from an aluminum coffee measure. It works just as well, but lacks the ladle's wooden handle, and must be held with a potholder as the heat reaches the end of the handle before it is clear of the melting pot.

No matter how carefully we work, some lead overflows, so we do our pouring over an old jeweler's bench Bill found in a dilapidated "swap and shop" establishment on the outskirts of the city. The "bench" is actually a shallow box about two feet square, six inches high on three sides and an inch high at the front. It is of solid old oak, lined with a floor of copper that catches and contains the hot tin of our work as it once caught the gold spilled in the making of lures of another sort. Almost any metal or asbestos lined box can serve as a work area.

*All manner of
strange devices
whose use,
just now,
escapes us
but which we
collect and
treasure
because they
are part of the
wonderful
paraphernalia
of the hunt.*

*His lure
and decoy
making have
grown beyond
the melt
and pour
simplicity
of his
lead soldier
days.*

The most important implement of all is the mold into which the tin is cast. If the shape of the lure is not perfect, then all lure-making efforts are worse than wasted. They will actually hamper later fishing success. We have dozens of molds of every kind. The simplest are Bill's experimental plaster models. These are used for small batches (up to five at most) of unusual shapes. First the shape is carved in wood, then an empty herring tin is filled to the top with orthopedic plaster and the prototype (which has been greased) pressed in. If the lure is flat on one side, the flat side is up, and the mold is ready as soon as the plaster dries. If the lure has ridges on both sides, a top mold will have to be made as well. The top mold is made by encircling the herring can with stiff paper extending about an inch and a quarter above the can's top. The paper will wrap quite snugly around the herring can's rounded corners. Then the plaster, which by then has dried with the lure still in it, and the lure are greased and another layer of plaster poured in up to the level of the top of the paper. When that plaster dries, the two halves of the mold can be separated and the lure removed.

If a one-piece mold is all that is required, it need only have a groove filed in for the hook ring holder after the prototype is removed and it is ready to use. If a two-piece mold is necessary, a little more work must be done. First a passage must be filed through the plaster at the lure's head for the tin to be poured into the mold. This passage should have a funnel shape and is best made by filing away from the lure body toward the outer edge of the plaster. Next a guide must be filed in the bottom mold for the wire base of the hook ring. This will, of course, correspond to the sort of ring material being used. Finally, small vents must be filed to allow the hot trapped air to escape, or it will cause bubble packs in the lure body. These vents are one-file-stroke grooves in the plaster that line the sides of the lure. They run out to the edge of the plaster, slanting up toward the lure's head. If all scoring and filing can be done with the can intact, Bill leaves it on, as it lends strength to the delicate plaster. Since the paper does not do much to prevent chipping or fracturing, the shallower side of the lure is on the paperbound half of the mold so that the unsupported plaster has fewer thin sections.

When Bill is ready to cast, he warms the insides of the molds over low heat, inserts the hook ring, then clamps both halves together with rubber bands. The mold is always filled with one smooth pouring of tin, as stopping in mid-lure allows half the tin to harden (it solidifies instantly) and the lure will either come out of the mold in two halves, or split along the line between the two batches of tin the first time a fish takes a tug at it. Just the thought of a monster bass getting away with the hook half of a lure while we reel in the other end instead of reeling in the fish keeps our casting smooth and consistent.

If one of the experimental lures turns out to be a real fish-getter or we decide to make our own version of a favorite commercial lure (filed down or built up with clay to work our improvements), the mold is made of plastic steel instead of plaster, and since, by then, several lures of the type we want are on hand, several lures go into the medium to make a multiple mold.

In addition to our own molds we also use some commercially made molds and a few antiques we've found. The commercial molds are

of two sorts: the standard items available from a number of instrument companies, and custom molds made by artists' casting services to conform to a model we supply. The standard molds are excellent lure makers, and generally reasonable. The bronze custom models are considerably more expensive and are not practical unless a lot of lures are needed fast.

The only time we've ever used a custom-made mold was the year the bass and blues were hitting baby flounder and one of Bill's experiments was the only successful lure on the beach. We had a multiple unit made up and our fishing friends equipped in a week. The antiques are the easiest molds to use. Each has a two-piece bronze body, with hinges at one side, handles on the other. We only need to set the hook eye wire, close the handles, pour the tin, release the handles, and be ready to set a wire again. We've found these treasures in some peculiar spots. The best, which makes six various-sized lures at once, was being used as a candy maker two hundred miles from the nearest salt water. But no matter what trade they are engaged in when we rescue them, the old lure makers slip back into their rightful roles with no trouble at all. The baitfish their products imitate haven't changed since the molds were struck, so the lures they yield are as useful as those from the best molds of today.

Most attractive of all the equipment used in hunting are the decoys used for duck and geese. Decoys can be simple stamped plastic shells, but the best of them transcend the utilitarian concept of hunting tools and become genuine art objects. As the skill of decoy carving has become recognized as an early native sculptural form, the works of the old craftsmen are collected by people who have never seen a duck blind, and the stools of Kellum, Corwin, Whittaker and the other master carvers of our area are generally considered to be too valuable to gun over.

The birds are usually displayed as primitive representational art, but this classification is only half correct. The artists were not untutored in their art—it was transmitted within families and regions for generations, with definite and evolving conventions of form and stool within each school. Very few of the schools (or regional patterns of convention) attempted to duplicate the actual shape or color of the fowl for which the decoy was intended, but rather tried to convey the impression of the bird when seen from certain angles and distances.

In the 1880s and 1890s, the era of massive flocks and massive kills, market hunters and gunning clubs maintained vast rafts of these exquisite decoys on Long Island's Great South Bay. At times hundreds of wooden birds would be set out for a single hunt for the millions-strong flocks of ducks and geese that wintered on the bay.

The decoys of this area were of two main types, with hollow and cork bodies. Bill and I find that the hollow-bodied birds bob around too much, but grab up every old cork duck we can find. Unfortunately very few survive, for these beautiful objects were tools of a knockabout sport and most were eventually lost, waterlogged or battered beyond recognition.

Still, there are a few to be found—the beach yields one every few years and scouting the local church bazaars can turn up one or two. Luck and persistence over the years have helped us assemble a small raft of black cork ducks, a number of solid-bodied Canada geese and an assortment of individual decoys. We've also collected some old rail decoys, and set them out when we go after ducks or geese in keeping with the local custom of having a few sand birds on hand to reinforce the impression of safety given by the waterfowl stools..

Our antique raft was a bit too small to be effective, so we decided to add to it with efforts of our own. Our first attempts were inspired by a waterlogged balsa raft we found on the beach. We got it home, dried it out and went to work. The raft was made of layers of balsa glued and doweled together and covered with canvas. Bill stripped off the fabric and cut the wood into sixteen nine-inch-square pieces each two and a half feet long. By planning his cuts carefully, Bill was able to get the rectangles intact without re-glueing or pegging.

We used our favorite antique as a model, and hacked out six rough body shapes with a sharp hatchet. Then we worked in stages to remove layers of wood, each step leaving a smoother surface than the one before. Hand knife, rasp and sandpaper shaped and refined the shape until our six bodies were nearly twins of their model.

White pine was carved into heads and necks in various feeding or resting poses and doweled through the balsa to the white pine keel we epoxied to the bottom. The whittling demanded fastidious attention to line and form. Our art required it even if the geese might not. The next step was one in which the stringent demands of craft and game coincided: painting.

Although the geese would not object to our decoys being twice goose size, a misapplied cheek patch might keep a flock away. Great care and practiced skill is essential, for decoys get only one coat of paint. That coat is drawn into the wood leaving its color, but not its gloss, on the surface. If more paint were applied, the feathery appearance of the first coat would be lost forever as a hard surface formed on the now-primed wood.

The birds' chest and body is painted dove grey, with white behind. The wings folded on the back and the head and neck are black, with a band of white running under the chin from cheek to cheek. The half dry wings are daubed with grey crescent stipples to imitate the natural plumage.

When we had finished our half dozen Canada geese we put them into action with their older brethren. It was impossible to distinguish our handiwork from our prized antiques when we set out the raft, and we crouched down in the blind in happy anticipation of the rewards of our labors winging in in flocks. They never came. After an hour afloat our new stools began to slip sideways or lopsided, and rode the waves in a most un-gooselike manner. Every few minutes one would have an extra weight tacked here or there to correct its posture, but they were well on their way to becoming a fleet of submarine geese when we called it a day. Keels were replaced with dowel spike legs, and our raft was converted to a field flock, which it has been, with great success, ever since.

The challenge of making floating decoys to match the best of our antiques was too great to pass up, and soon we were at work again, this time with pressed cork, to multiply our black duck raft. The technique was the same as for the geese—progressively finer shapings of the cork body with hatchet, knife, rasp and sandpaper, a white pine head and neck and keel doweled into the body. The painting was much simpler, for pressed cork is exactly the right color for black duck decoys, and only a small fleck of purple is necessary. The head and neck are tan, with markings of the same burnt umber as the cork.

These worked so well that soon we went into mass production. A local carpentry shop made up ten dozen white pine head blanks and we set about whittling them into shape, then carved ten dozen cork block bodies.

It seemed the work went all too fast. Our basement had become an island of time from another time, a magic anachronism that was just ten steps down from the world of present time. The sweet clean smell of shaven pine mingled with clean smelling chestnut as the mellow sounds of wood mallet striking wooden chisel shaft and old sharp steel chipping yielding wood gave steady beat to the music of sandpaper and rasp. A carpenter's workbench almost a century old held vises, mallets, chisels, and rasps it might have held when new. Old tools that knew their craft far better than the hands that held them seemed at times to guide those hands in copying what was perhaps the very work the tools had done a carpenter's lifetime past.

We carved out rails, and their wild cherrywood beaks were oven baked, then singed for natural color. Great Canada geese appeared in silhouette, with heads on hinges to position in the field. Only in these simplest of all decoys did modern time return, for they are sawn from masonite for working ease and lightest weight. But even here the rare old finds, the antique decoys, set the scale and pattern of our birds, and set the craftsman standard of our work.

One small room of our country house looks like an Army-Navy surplus store, and well it might, for almost every item in it passed through one on its way to us. Two large closets bulge with clothes designed to meet far higher requirements than the standards of the hunt. Storm coats, jackets, parkas all made to stand the rigors of the arctic are there for comfort on the coldest days. There are flight suits and long johns, trigger-finger mittens and khaki trousers, enough to outfit a couple or a dozen hunting guests.

The room itself holds bags, knapsacks, pouches and boxes to carry out our gear or bring back our catch. The webbing of our duck and goose blinds and the camouflage nets for their roofs and floor are piled among dozens of invaluable tools all stamped or printed with a black "U.S."

This military gear is all the finest to be had, and can be purchased at a fraction of a fraction of its real price. We have never been

unable to come up with the gear to help us overcome any conditions imaginable, thanks to our surplus store shopping. We even have equipment for conditions beyond our imaginations which were on special sale and we picked up "just in case."

That seems to be the way of all hunting paraphernalia. Its grace or its utility or just the simple pleasure of acquiring it at little or no cost to have around in case of some unlikely need has filled our country basement, an attic, a room, and now some city closets, too, with bigger flocks of wooden ducks than most of the flocks that fly, with hundreds of new tin lures each year to make up for the ten we lost, with clothes enough to outfit an expedition, though we seldom hunt with more than two or three guests. And with infra-red signal lamps, surveyors' tools, whaleboat oars and all manner of other strange devices whose use, just now, escapes us but which we collect and treasure because they are all part of the wondrous and wonderful paraphernalia of the hunt.

Chapter 16.

Memorabilia

The day was a dreary monochrome. Grey clouds poured grey sheets of rain through black air to make grey slush of the early snow. We had planned to go out for pheasant, but the forecast was for steady rain, and the birds would be roosting tight. It might have been a wasted day but for one special hunt we make when circumstances make other adventures impossible: the hunt for memorabilia.

Memorabilia takes many forms, from mounted heads to antique implements of the catch to the native crafts and old impedimenta of our hunting grounds. We pursue it around the areas surrounding our country house on Long Island, in our deer hunting territory in upstate New York, while after boar in North Carolina or trout in Pennsylvania. Although no area is so remote that it has not been scoured by antique hunters, all occasionally yield treasures, and delightful finds of less than exalted lineage are common everywhere.

That day we were on home ground, and decided to check out one of the old barns on our mental list of places to examine when we found the time. We put our shotguns in the trunk of the car just in case the weather cleared and were off. The barn stood alone near the road in a pasture. On the opposite side of the road were some frame houses, about fifty years old, twenty years younger than the barn.

We found the owner on our first attempt, in the largest, most rambling house of the irregular row. He matched his home in habit and appearance, a casually untidy giant whose casual untidyness had, in fifty years, wreaked havoc on his once elegant dwelling.

Flecks of paint hinted at the more recent colors that had adorned the mostly bare wood. A strangely intact bannister recalled a long vanished set of stairs, and a sagging porch roof implied that once there had been a porch. The inside was incredible. Whole rooms were filled with bundled papers. V-E Day's headlines must have still been there. Crates of decayed vegetables were neatly stacked in the living room, waiting to go to market, as they had waited since before the market closed almost a year past.

Our host explained that he had been a widower for almost thirty years, and had found that the orderly regularity of married life restricted his spirit, and so he remained a bachelor, free to clutter and collect and retain whatever most appealed to him. It seemed that our tastes were less than parallel, so we asked if we might

see the castoff things in his old barn. He was delighted to have us look, as the barn was "full of a lot of old junk" he wanted to get rid of. With a silent shudder at the thought of what *he* would call "old junk" we followed him across the road.

The waist-deep weeds in the field were littered with rusted farm implements and auto parts, but there was an approximation of a path winding through the clutter. The owner explained that selling half of the land beyond the road had left him with enough money to live and to pay the taxes on the field, and that after years of farming it he enjoyed owning it and just letting it sit there.

When we got to the barn we had some second thoughts. It seemed about to collapse (one portion already had), and we doubted that any find would be worth the risk of being buried in a heap of rotted pine laced with foot-square oak beams. But we had come this far, so we decided to brave it.

Strangely enough, the roof kept out the rain, even though the gaps in the siding let in enough light for us to see comfortably. The centerpiece of the place was an ancient tractor, and I had visions of it pulling the lawn mower around our grounds as Bill made straight for it. To my amazed relief, his interest was short lived, and he joined me in rummaging through a pile of furniture off in a corner.

. . . implements of the catch to the native crafts and impedimenta of our hunting grounds.

Apparently goats had once lived here, for most of the upholstery had been eaten, but one of the sofas had a very gracefully carved rosewood frame that was completely intact. Our host said that it had been quite good and quite expensive at one time and was worth, he thought, twenty-five dollars. We agreed to his price and began to wonder about ways and means of getting it to an old craftsman upholsterer in our village, when the man volunteered that he had expected us to do a little bargaining rather than agreeing to his first price, and so would throw in free delivery.

He backed an old pickup truck through the maze with well practiced deftness, then, before we could offer to help or protest, picked up the sofa and set it gently in the truck bed as if it had no weight at all.

His laugh at our amazement was delicious. Before we had recovered our senses he grabbed a small millstone from the floor and hoisted it over his head, relishing and reveling in his strength. The man was seventy-five if a day, and yet had lifted at least two hundred pounds above his head, and held it there, and laughed all the time he was doing it.

He invited us back to the house for tea, and we could tell that conversation, much more than the twenty-five dollars, was his price for the sofa. He was so remarkable that nothing could have dissuaded us even if we had to bring a piece of furniture from our living room for admission. The tea was strong and black, served in cups stained grey with grime. The man overflowed with vigor as he told us some tales of his vigorous life. We heard of flocks of ducks that blacked out the sky of long ago and guns long since illegal that brought down forty with one shot. We heard of liquor dropped from planes into a nearby lake, then gathered by midnight "fishermen" and taken to the local speakeasy. We heard how intolerable it had become since the neighborhood got crowded (those other four old houses on the half-mile stretch of road), and prissy housewives came by, it seemed most every year, to nag and scold and demand that he clean up.

We listened the day into dusk and then went home, leaving the address of the craftsman. The next weekend the upholsterer gave us an excited call. When I heard his nervous voice I was afraid the giant had taken a liking to his porch and carried it off to put under his porch roof, and would not have been too surprised if that had been the case. I was surprised by the actual reason for the excitement. Someone, he said, had dropped off a pile of rags and tatters and left it in our name, and that pile of rags and tatters was tacked to a signed Johnny Belter frame! The sofa the giant had said was once "quite good and quite expensive" was an original from the hand of one of the finest Victorian frame makers. There was no doubt about it, according to the old craftsman. The construction details, the grace of line, the traces of finish that remained on the wood, all confirmed the genuineness of the signature that was too good to be true. He said he had a bolt of fine white silk that he had saved for several years, and that he'd like to use it on this near-priceless piece. We knew his taste and skill enough to agree at once, and the exquisite result is now one of the prides of our city living room. But although we got a frame worth a few thousand dollars for twenty-five and an afternoon's attentive listening, the real treasure of that afternoon was the talk we listened to, and the many talks we have had since with the man whose answer when we asked if he knew what he had sold and if he really wanted to sell it was "Told you it was good. I bought it back in '31 from some folks who had a big place out here. Bad year for them. Good one for me. That was the year I ran a . . ."

Although we've never had a day quite like the one that gave us a rare antique and a rarer friend, almost all of our regular hunting grounds have yielded lovely things and lovely memories: two turn-of-the-century solid oak sleds, once used to haul maple sap in our upstate deer territory, now coffee tables in our country house; a prayer bench from a Smoky Mountain country church anxious to replace its rustic grace with a modern pew; massive butcher blocks for end tables, horse collars to frame mirrors, old tools and prints for decoration, all come from other uses and other eras, from grander or simpler times.

But these are only part of the memorabilia we collect. The hunts themselves provide the rest. A day spent stalking deer may not produce venison, but we are sure to find old antlers or giant pine cones on the forest floor. These are the decorations of our venison feasts. When the stalk has been successful the taxidermist gets the handsomest heads, and the fierce visages of bear and boar. A search for decoys led us to a collection of marsh birds mounted at the turn of the century. Six perfect domes of glass, the largest three feet high, keep dust from crowded aviaries of game birds, some long extinct, for all appearances alive and still, though dead and stuffed for nearly seventy years.

We mount our trophy fish ourselves (and save the fillets while doing it), a custom inaugurated by my first striped bass and followed with all super fish since then. It really is quite easy to commemorate and enjoy spectacular catches.

The pheasant hunt is the richest in game-derived memorabilia. The most beautiful birds are skinned and framed as pheasant pelts. The pelts can also be used as chair seats, throw pillows, or miniature throws. The framed pelts are our favorites, and they are especially attractive when a brace, a male and female, are done as a pair. We prefer them in old Victorian frames with convex glass, on antique velvet backgrounds in rich earth colors to provide a deep counterpoint to the pheasants' brilliant plumage.

The plumage is the basis for some of our favorite finery: evening shoes, hatbands, vests, frames, throw pillows and rugs. When plucking the birds we set aside all marked feathers, and clip off the down at the end, being careful not to clip the quill itself. Those feathers, some thread or glue, and a shape to be covered are all that is needed.

We occasionally mount a brace of pheasant whole, instead of just preserving the pelt. Rather than mounting them standing in awkward "lifelike" poses, however, we hang them as they hang while curing, and mount them on an oaken plank.

The mounted heads of bear and deer and boar are seconded by their cured skins: the bear a rug before the fireplace, the deer in buckskin jackets, the boar a rough pigskin for wallets and gloves that sound a note of primitive wildness through their civilized shapes and forms. Deer feet are coat racks and shotgun racks and fishing rod racks, while four powerful black boar feet cradle the two powerful Remingtons of the boar and bear hunt.

Even the harvest of the jellies and liqueurs have their derivative harvests of memorabilia. Rose petals not needed for Rose-Petal Jelly are made into Potpourri, and aromatic bayberries gathered in the fields on the way back from collecting wild cherries envelop our apartment in their delightful fragrance all winter long.

No matter what we hunt, or where we hunt it, we feel obliged to get the very most from the experience, and to make the most possible use of every imaginable by-product. Of course, we always eat our catch, but to waste any usable part of our bag would violate our belief that our adventures are not only permissible, but, in fact, essential, in that they are vivid reminders that all life is based on other life-taking, and that those lives that sustain life must never be taken in vain. That awareness compels us to make maximum use of flesh and fur and feathers, but more, it demands that we appreciate the deep and basic satisfactions of our shared meeting and mastering of nature's challenges that is the spirit of the catch and the feast.

Making and Collecting Mementos

182

Preserving Pheasant Pelts

Carefully *skin* pheasant by slitting skin from neck down breastbone with sharp pointed blade. Pull skin up, inserting fingers under skin; apply upward pressure to separate skin from flesh.

To cure the pelt, coat the inside with a very thick layer of borax. Place undisturbed (borax-coated side up) in airtight plastic bag where no moisture can penetrate. Allow 3 to 4 weeks for curing. Then shake off borax and allow skin to "air" in fresh air and sunshine for several days, taking care to bring pelt indoors before sunset each day.

Framed Pelts

Find oval convex frame from early 1900's and line it with beautiful antique velvet in rich deep colors such as burgundy, rose or deep forest green.

Center pheasant skin in the frame, using straight pins to secure. Place tail feathers in place with tacking pins. Replace glass and frame.

Decorating with Pheasant Feathers

Evening clothes, hats, and many home accessories can be magnificently transformed by the application of pheasant feathers.

Pluck pheasant, carefully reserving all marked feathers—virtually every feather of the pheasant!

To decorate evening shoes, wooden and cloth objects, and leather picture frames, clip the downy section and tip of quill from each feather, dip just the quill end into contact cement, and apply feathers in rows, overlapping so that only the part with markings is visible. Continue row after row until object is completely feather-covered.

Feathers can be sewn to hatbands and hats for a marvelous effect. For a hatband, trim heavy grosgrain ribbon or felt to 1½-inch width and desired length, allowing for an overlap when it goes around hat.

Do *not* clip feathers at quill end—just clip off downy fluff.

Place one feather at a time on band.

Begin stitching with needle and doubled cotton thread.

Overlap feathers well up to markings to ensure that finished band will have no cracks showing quill or stitches.

Continue one feather at a time, overlapping on all sides until a luxuriant slightly convex feather band is completed.

For a hat, take a favorite felt hat base, preferably an old hat of fedora, helmet or pillbox shape (perennially fashionable). Stitch on marked feathers, one at a time, in a uniform clockwise manner, overlapping feathers row upon row.

If the hat has a brim, apply feathers inside of brim as well as out. This project will not be completed at one sitting, but can be picked up as desired.

For a man's vest, cover velvet or silk vest front with festive applique of marked pheasant feathers, sewing on one feather at a time in carefully overlapping rows, narrowing or filling in as contour demands.

Velvet pillows are handsome with feathers sewn in random patterns, overall, or on the face side only.

An unusual and very elegant throw rug can be created on a round, oblong, square or rectangular base by sewing on pheasant feathers one at a time. Carefully overlap each feather, row after row.

These larger areas offer greater design opportunity for working circular, oval, mosaic and other patterns.

For an exotic touch for a living room or study, save long tail feathers from five or six pheasants.

Place in wooden mortar (7 to 8 inches high) for unique permanent desk bouquet.

The tail feathers from two or three birds can be made simply into a feather duster. Bind the feathers together with a sturdy string at base.

Buy a handle hollowed out on one end. Try for fit. If quills do not fit snugly, bind more string around feathers. Apply contact cement to bound end of feathers and to hollow end of handle. Wait 10 minutes, insert feathers firmly, and allow to set at least overnight.

Dried Roses

Bind stems of 12 roses with rubber band. Do not remove leaves. Hang in dry, airy place for 3 to 4 weeks. Roses will be completely "cured" and last a lifetime, retaining a beautiful, somewhat faded color and delicate fragrance.

Cut away rubber band and arrange flowers in a silver or crystal vase or in a natural clay flowerpot.

184 Pomander Balls

1 large navel orange   *2 tablespoons cinnamon*
⅛ pound large whole cloves   *2 tablespoons orris root*

Prick orange with nutpick at ⅛-inch intervals, making 5 to 6 small holes at a time. Insert whole cloves, allowing the heads to stud surface of orange. Repeat in rows around orange until entire sphere is closely covered with cloves.

Combine cinnamon and orris root in brown paper bag. Place clove-studded orange in bag and shake vigorously until orange is thickly coated with mixture.

Insert 4 sturdy toothpicks into orange as legs. Stand orange on toothpick legs on a little plate in dry, airy place and allow to remain *undisturbed* for 3 to 5 weeks. Do not touch or handle orange during curing period as it becomes very soft and would break while the juice is being absorbed into the clove stems.

When cured, orange will be very hard and completely hollow inside, and will exude a heady perfume fragrance for life.

Bleached Artichokes

Place 8 large artichokes on a fine mesh screen and dry in bright sunlight for 3 to 4 weeks. Bring indoors at sunset each day and keep in dry place.

When cured, artichokes will be wheat-colored, almost weightless and permanently preserved. Use for centerpiece arrangements combined with sunbleached deer antlers in a handsome wicker basket or in a silver, porcelain or crystal bowl.

When cured, artichokes will be wheat-colored, almost weightless and permanently preserved. Use for centerpiece arrangements combined with sunbleached deer antlers in a handsome wicker basket or in a silver, porcelain or crystal bowl.

Sunbleached Deer Antlers

Individual, unmatched deer antlers can be bought rather inexpensively in almost any rural and in many city curio shops.

Soak 6 or more deer antlers in a mild Clorox and water solution for approximately 2 hours. Remove from solution and allow to bleach in the sun for an entire summer. A mild Clorox solution can be poured over antlers from time to time during curing. Horns need not be brought indoors during bleaching process. When completely weathered, use as sculpture or in centerpiece with bleached artichokes.

Potpourri

2 quarts rose petals
¼ pound dried lavender
¼ pound dried patchouli branches
¼ pound cinnamon sticks
2 ounces whole cloves
2 ounces powdered orris root
Whole dried rosebuds

Dry rose petals on fine-mesh wire rack for 3 weeks in dry, well-ventilated place. Rake over with hands each day, turning petals over.

When completely dried, place in large silver or crystal bowl or in handsome leather antique hatbox, adding the lavender, patchouli branches, cinnamon sticks, cloves and orris root.

Add whole dried rosebuds for added color and dimension, taking care to balance any sizable addition with the proper amount of corresponding other ingredients. Potpourri will provide an exotic fragrance for a lifetime.

Dried Flowers Collage

Dry an attractive assortment of field flowers, proceeding as with dried roses. When completely preserved, prepare a framed velvet surface, preferably of a soft, muted color. Arrange flowers artistically, using a good fabric adherent for best results.

Horse Collar Mirror

Curiously enough, old horse collars can be found with regularity in curio shops in the city as well as through the countryside.

Rub saddle soap well into the old leather, buff, and repeat until leather glows.

Have mirror cut to shape of flat side of horse collar and attach with heavy-duty mirror screw clips by screwing into leather rim and catching edge of mirror in clip.

Attach heavy-duty screw eyes into leather rim to desired height for hanging and string sturdy wire through. Fasten at edges by twisting wire ends.

Paint wooden traces as desired (deep red or green are exceptionally effective). If traces are adorned with brass and have brass knobs at top, polish brass to dazzling brightness. Hang horse collar mirror and adjust traces into position.

Deer Horn Chairs

Use any small chair with upholstered seat. Remove legs.

Prepare 4 evenly matched antlers (of at least 4 points per individual antler) by drilling hole at base to open for insertion of hardwood dowel. Have dowel shaped for a very snug fit.

Drill corresponding hole in chair frame and insert other end of dowel. With chair in upside-down position, force heavy-duty bonding cement around fitting.

When completely dry, stand chair upright and apply bonding cement around dowel at edge of horn. Massage cement well into crevices. Allow to dry completely.

Bind the joints with leather sleeves in black or a color complementing the upholstery.

Duck or Goose Decoy Lamp

Drill hole through decoy and wire as for standard lamp. Mount on handsome wooden base by putting screws through base to decoy. Cover bottom of base with velvet or baize.

Block and Tackle Lamp

Tap out the pin that holds sheaves of block in place. String standard lamp wiring through hollow but heavy metal tube (sturdy curtain rod will do), of size identical with removed pin. Insert wired tube through block and sheaves and attach to roughhewn or finished wooden base with screws. Cover bottom with base of can-vas or baize.

Decorative Old Farm Implements

Every drive through rural areas can yield a find of treasures in old implements and tools which can become unique home decorations: for example, scythes, feather forks, pitchforks, saws, axes. Gild blade, tongs, or other metal surfaces. Wax, varnish or paint the wooden handles, or cover with cloth or wallpaper. Hang in group.

Butcher Blocks

Even if they are in a ravaged or weary condition, authentic old butcher blocks are handsome tables for town or country. Scour with a mild solution of caustic salt. Allow to dry thoroughly. Treat with repeated applications of paste wax, rubbing and buffing after each application. When used as living room end tables, pile them high with delightful clutter: old wooden handmade reels, carved railbirds, old clam knives, antique lures, planes, small blocks and tackle, and of course decoy and block and tackle lamps.

Beaded Curtains

Unique beads are often available in out-of-the-way shops. Hand-made, irregularly shaped tubular mosaics are very effective and colorful when combined with small round black wooden beads with accompanying flat wooden discs which are raised slightly in the center.

Soak the wood beads and discs in a solution of paint remover for about 20 minutes. Rinse in cold water and scrub the mass of beads at random. This will produce a marvelously aged appearance.

Using a heavy waxed linen string (with end triple-waxed for easier threading), string one disc, one round wooden bead, continue for 4 to 10 inches, then punctuate with large tubular mosaic bead. Repeat, keeping intervals between mosaics irregular, until desired length is reached.

String as many lengths as are required. Using each preceding length as a guideline, string each length so that mosaics will fall interspersed irregularly throughout the entire beaded curtain. Allow a 5-inch piece of string at one end for fastening onto the wooden strip from which beads will hang.

When desired number of lengths have been strung for each side of curtain, drill small holes at ¾-inch intervals through a strip of rosewood 2 x 1 inch in thickness and the proper length for the curtain. Thread excess string of each completed length through hole. Secure at top to strips of hardwood ¾ inch long and ¼ inch thick.

When both sides of curtain have been strung, measure distance in between and string short lengths for a center valance. The valance (4- to 10-inch lengths) should form pointed scallops. Begin at very center and work out design to each end.

Hang beaded curtain by resting rosewood base on 4 to 6 flat-headed spikes driven deeply into wall or surface from which beaded curtain is to hang. If curtain will hang from ceiling, rosewood base must be screwed into ceiling.

Norseman Chairs

The following method can be followed for cured animal hides of almost any kind: bear or deer, or steer, tiger, zebra, etc. The chairs themselves can be antique Dante chairs or their modern and very inexpensive counterparts—the ubiquitous director's chairs.

Use the existing seat saddle and back strip for a template; or if you are working with frame only, make pattern to chair's dimensions. Trace pattern onto reverse side of pelt. Cut skin from reverse side with knife blade *up* (this will ensure edges luxuriantly fringed with fur and no raveling). Secure skin to Dante chairs with large button tacks (antique, if possible). For director's chairs, secure skins as you would with canvas.

Attic Sleepers

Almost every old attic can be counted on to yield wondrous things from many places and eras, from grander or simpler times.

Embroidered pure silk Spanish shawls—flamboyantly beautiful, vividly embroidered on pure rare silk and lavishly fringed—need only to be dry-cleaned (and perhaps mended inconspicuously) to serve as festive game-feast tablecloths.

Mellow old musical instruments, such as a mandolin, mandola, cello or bass fiddle, can be restored by rubbing lemon oil gently into the old wood. Hang on wall or display smaller instruments on a table.

To restore an old moose head, clean matted, dusty hair with wig cleaner. A quart of solution is required. Dip scrubbing brush into solution and scrub down in the direction the hair grows. Repeat until thoroughly clean. Allow to dry thoroughly. Wax and buff antlers. Brush hair when dry with ordinary hair brush. Hang in your dining room or living room as "now" art.

Antebellum leather hatboxes, relined with velvet or fur, can be handsome for holding Potpourri.

Clean leather thoroughly. Remove old muslin or silk lining and make template. Cut velvet, deer hide, bearskin, fox, etc. to pattern, cover with a good fabric adherent and apply to inside of hatbox. Varnish exterior leather.

Little game birds or exquisite song birds on delicate, natural branches under glass domes are Victorian conceits that are not as fragile and unredeemable as might at first appear. Clean feathers of each bird with wig cleaner, using toothbrush. Wax beaks, re-touch and repair feet if required with molding clay and oil colors. In the twenties there was scarcely a family in America who didn't have a bear rug *somewhere*. Scrub bear rug with wig cleaner. Allow to dry, and brush. If fur lacks luster spray with a lanolin hair spray preparation or rub brilliantine in the palms of the hands and massage through fur. Repair tongue, if needed, by applying a layer of molding clay; coat over with household wax. Tint with oil colors. If paws require repairs, use black monkey, skunk or other available fur. Claws and fangs could be approximated at a five-and-ten jewelry counter and applied with molding clay.

Decorative Deer Feet

Cut deer feet to desired length below knee bone.

Remove marrow by inserting stick into the center of bone.

Wash in strong soap and water.

Mix ½ box borax in bucket of cold water. Soak deer feet for 10 days. As well as preserving feet, this moth-proofs them forever.

Remove feet from borax solution and bend to desired shape.

Allow to cure for 14 days in cool, dry place.

For best drying results drive nails into a board, placing deer feet upright on nails.

When completely dry, melt lead to molten liquid and back-fill center hole in bone to 1 inch below top.

Hammer 2-inch wood screwhead to square, insert into bone with threads above the surface and fill in with molten lead.

When set, rub hoofs and dewclaws with paste wax, and buff on electric buffer to desired gloss.

Screw into wooden plaques or directly into wall areas as desired.

Mounting a Hanging Pheasant

Trace pheasant on sturdy paper; make outlines from several positions before skinning. Fill in the details of distinct feather tracts: the neck, shoulder scapulars, rump, wing, flank and breast plumage areas. After drawing a side view of pheasant body, draw an oval outline extending just beyond the natural outline. This will be the pattern for the excelsior body.

It is best to work on a work bench, preferably in a cellar. Have ample quantity of borax on hand for absorbing juices and blood and to keep the skin supple. Plug all cavities and shot holes with absorbent cotton.

Make an incision the full length of the abdomen and breast with a sharp scalpel. Cut only through the skin and not into the carcass of bird. Peel skin by inserting fingers carefully beneath loosened edges. Start from incision and peel skin away from the breast. Use borax liberally as you peel, sprinkling it onto skin and meat. Sever the knees with a cartilage knife or scissors.

Set pheasant on its breast and cut through the rectum, tail meat and bone. Avoid puncturing skin on top of tail. Continue peeling. Use scalpel to free skin where necessary. Cut through the shoulder joints and peel the skin over the head. Pull ear linings out with knitting needle or tweezers. Cut eyelid linings away, clip close to the skull. Cut off neck at base of skull. Clean brain cavity, removing brain, eyeballs and fat. Sprinkle borax into cavity while cleaning, then coat the skull heavily with extra borax. Sprinkle the now free skin liberally with borax and scrape off all fat and meat. Peel skin back over the legs. Sever the tendons and clean meat away from leg bones. Rub borax on bones. Sprinkle over with extra borax.

Peel the skin off wings down to the elbows, sever the tendons and clean meat from bones. Make an incision along the middle of the underside of the forearm and clean out meat. Coat the surface with borax, working into crevices. Re-scrape entire skin surface; coat with thick layer of borax and rub into skin. Wash skin in a soap and borax solution. Gently squeeze out skin, then wrap in several layers of Turkish towels to absorb all excess moisture. Dust with borax and preen feathers with toothpicks with ends covered with a bit of cotton.

Skin must be kept moist (in dampened towels) during mounting. Turn head inside out and wrap excelsior over the top and sides of the skull. Fill the eye sockets with excelsior. Pull skin back into position.

Starting with a large wad of excelsior, wrap additional strips around until a pear-shaped body is formed. Wrap with twine; reshape with strips of excelsior where needed, finish with twine. Compare with sketch of pheasant for accuracy.

Use wire coat hangers to make wires for leg, tail, wing, and neck. Sharpen ends. Cut extra long lengths for working; excess will be tucked in or clipped off. Neck wire must be twice as long as the artificial body. Sharpen end and insert through body, leaving ample wire at top for fashioning neck. Bend back excess wire at bottom and tuck it up inside body. Wind excelsior around wire to create neck. Keep the winding tight and even. When proper shape is achieved, wrap neck with thread. Allow more width at top of neck for pushing up into the brain cavity.

Attach neck to body with small pins. Insert the wing wire along the back of the elbows until it exits at wing tips. Attach wire to forearm bone with thread and stuff cavity smoothly with excelsior. Stitch incision.

Insert leg wires through the back of legs, allowing only short lengths to remain above knees for making "drumsticks." Tie the wire to the bone. Wrap excelsior drumstick-fashion around wire, then wrap with thread. Pull leg skin back into place.

Push tip of neck wire through neck (carefully so as not to puncture skin). Continue up through the mouth and clip off excess. Settle brain cavity onto top of neck and bring skin back over. Aim wing wires into opposite sides of the body and bend excess into place. Partially arrange body skin.

Insert leg wires into opposite sides of body and bend excess to fit. Insert tail wire and adjust tail snugly in place. Sew up breast incision.

Since pheasant will hang by its feet, the position is not difficult to arrange. Preen plumage by dipping cotton-wrapped toothpicks into a liquid dry-cleaning preparation for wigs. Allow to dry, then brush gently with sable-hair eyebrow brush. Prepare a mixture of papier-mâché; fill bottom of feet and eye sockets. Insert glass eyes into place. Drive a flat spike into a handsome piece of weathered driftwood, and hang pheasant from spike by leather game-bird thong. Bird can dry as it hangs, and therefore can be hung at once.

Mounting a Striped Bass

Place the fish on a dampened towel with the more perfect side down. With a very sharp knife make an incision right down the middle, from tail fin to gill at shoulder. Make cross incision along end of tail fin. Lay edges back and cut through the base of fin bones with heavy snippers.

Cut the fin bone roots free from body. Remove the skin by carefully working your fingers between skin and body. Do not bend skin. Keep it wet and take every care to retain scales.

When entire body is free of skin, use heavy snippers to free body from shoulder girdle. (Fillet body and refrigerate for eating). Do not cut through the chest attachment at throat of fish.

Use a spoon with a serrate tip and a scraping scalpel for removing cheek muscle and flesh. Remove eyeballs. Clean out the brain cavity. Leave skull whole but nip out all gristle and fat material. Slit skin under tongue and scrape out all fat. Prepare a solution of borax and strong brown laundry soap.

Sliver the soap into chips and knead with powdered borax. Massage this mixture thoroughly but carefully inside fish skin, head and brain cavity. This will help enormously in releasing the clinging flesh, which must be scraped out thoroughly, and will also aid preservation. Keep outside of skin (opened out flat) on wet towel at all times to keep it pliable and to preserve scales.

Sprinkle ample dry powdered borax on gills and inside mouth, rubbing it in carefully. Then wash gills with borax water. Dust again with borax.

Prepare two thicknesses of muslin or linen (an old sheet or table-cloth is good) and place flattened fish form on top. Trace all around fish from shoulder to base of fin with soft heavy black marking pencil. Cut out tracing. Now put entire fish skin into a bucket containing 4 gallons of cold water and 2 cups borax. Soak 2 to 4 hours.

Make papier-mâché from prepared mixture, adding the specified amount of water. Spread papier-mâché on one thickness of cloth, about ¾ inch thick. Place second fish-shaped cloth on top and sew together with basting stitches. Remove fish skin from borax solution and pat carefully with Turkish towel. Place show side on a damp towel, and fit papier-mâché form evenly inside flattened fish skin. It should exactly duplicate shape and size of fish skin. Using curved, heavy needle, thimble, and sturdy waxed linen thread, begin sewing together. Catch the basted form and fish skin with each stitch. Sew an inch and a half, then pack sawdust into cavity, pressing it down tightly with a wooden pestle.

Continue sewing an inch and a half at a time, packing in sawdust at each interval. About midway, check to determine if there is enough girth to your fish—stuff in more sawdust if needed. When sewing and stuffing is completed, shape with hands for final finishing touches.

Smooth any bumps. Insert piece of balsa between skull and throat points and stuff cheeks with excelsior. Adjust tongue and block it into position.

Cut out cardboard tracings of fins and attach to fins with paper clips. Dampen fins with wet sponge. Wipe entire fish with denatured alcohol. Allow fish to dry in well-ventilated dry area for approximately three weeks. Keep fins dampened throughout the drying process.

When thoroughly dry cut three quarter-sized holes above the seam on the back side of fish. Shake out all sawdust.

Fill eye socket with papier-mâché and set glass eye into place.

Place fish on handsome mounting board. Make markings corresponding to three holes in fish. Drill out holes in board. Place fish in position. Insert a toggle screw through board into each of the three holes.

Wipe fish skin with denatured alcohol. Let dry.

Give entire fish a thin, even coat of shellac. Allow to dry completely. Do not paint or color in any way. The natural appearance, although slightly yellow, is by far the most attractive.

Gear

All of our hunts and harvests and their attendant feasts can be accomplished with a minimum of gear and a well-equipped kitchen. Specialized guns, tackle and clothing are convenient for those pursuits which become favorite and frequent avocations, but the list below provides a guideline to basic gear for sampling all the sensations of the catch and the feast.

Twelve-gauge automatic shotgun with modified choke (deer, Canada goose, pheasant, wild turkey, duck and small game)
Center fire rifle of 6 mm. or larger caliber (deer, boar and bear)
Appropriate ammunition for choice of firearm
Leather gun case, soft unlined leather or canvas
Binoculars (deer, striped bass and bluefish)
Non-sinkable flashlight (lake fish, striped bass, duck and frogs)
Bird shooter hunting boots, lightweight and reasonably waterproof (pheasant, boar and bear, wild turkey and small game)
Heavy-duty insulated, waterproof hunting boots (deer, goose and duck)
Insulated long underwear (deer, goose, duck and late fall striped bass)
Olive drab parka, quilted down-lined (goose and duck)
Heavy-duty, water-repellent olive drab canvas trousers (goose and duck)
Fur-lined hats with ear muffs, olive drab (goose and duck)
Rubber hip boots (goose, duck, trout and striped bass)
Shooting gloves, olive drab (goose, duck, deer and small game)
Heavy pure wool socks
Compass (deer, boar and bear, wild turkey)
Duffel bag of water-repellent cotton duck
Portable duck and goose blind of reeds and marsh grass woven into khaki lattice or chicken wire
8 to 12 duck decoys, cork or plastic
8 to 12 Canada goose decoys (masonite silhouettes)
Duck, goose and turkey calls
Woolen shirt
Turtleneck woolen sweater
Red plaid woolen cap with earflaps (deer, boar and bear)
Red plaid heavy-duty wool hunting breeches and jacket (deer, boar and bear)
Hunting knife
Brier-resistant game coat with matching canvas-front trousers (pheasant, turkey, small game)
Loop game carrier (all birds and small game)
Slicker suit (bluefish, striped bass, deer (in rain), lake fish)
Deck shoes or rubber boots
Turtle trap, hoop net or chicken-wire box construction
2 metal jig molds (for making lures)
Chisel, rasp and hatchet (for making decoys)
Clam rake and basket
Lobster trap
Seining net
Gigging spear (frogs and flat saltwater fish)
Hand trap and clay pigeons

Especially for Striped Bass

10-foot Fiberglas surf rod
Spinning reel carrying 300 yards of 15-pound test line
Gaff
2 surface poppers
2 metal jigs
2 swimming plugs
12-inch wire leaders, number 8
Garrison belt
Stringer
Portable gasoline lantern

Especially for Lake Fishing

6½-foot lightweight spinning rod
Lightweight spinning reel holding 200 yards of 6-pound test line
3 spinners
3 surface plugs
3 spoons
3 swimming plugs
Tackle box
Landing net (lake fish and trout)
Clippers (lake fish, trout, striped bass and bluefish)
Scaler-knife combination (virtually all fishing sports)
Polaroid glasses, green or grey (lake fish and trout)

Especially for Trout

7-foot split bamboo or Fiberglas fly rod
Lightweight, single-action fly reel
Floating and sinking fly lines
2 dozen assorted wet and dry flies
Fly boxes, compartmentalized with windows
Leaders, 7½ to 9 feet
Line dressing
Insect repellent
Creel, wicker or canvas
Fly vest with ventilated game pocket
Trout fisherman's knife and clip

Especially for Bluefish

*6-foot sturdy Fiberglas boat rod with heavy butt, marked with gradings in order
that line can be measured out to correct depth*
Star-drag boat reel (large handle) with 200 yards 30-pound test monofilament line
Large canvas tote bag
Fishing pliers

Especially for Preparing the Feasts

Large fish poacher with rack
Swedish fish smoker with sack of pulverized wood
Large cast-iron kettle

The Catch
And
The Feast

Extra large clam steamer
Large tin-lined shallow baking pan
Extra large tin-lined copper skillet
A collection of casseroles in assorted sizes
4 earthen crocks (1-, 2-, 4- and 8-gallon sizes)
Large-mouthed earthen jug (2-gallon size)
Garlic press
2 wooden spoons
Sugar thermometer
Large deep-frying unit
Jelly bag, cheesecloth, mason jars and wax
An ample supply of red and dry white wine

196